LETTERS OF
OLIVER GOLDSMITH

T0370856

THE
COLLECTED LETTERS
OF
OLIVER GOLDSMITH

Edited by

KATHARINE C. BALDERSTON, Ph.D.

Assistant Professor of English Literature
at Wellesley College

CAMBRIDGE
AT THE UNIVERSITY PRESS
1928

TO

Professor Chauncey Brewster Tinker

CAMBRIDGE
UNIVERSITY PRESS

University Printing House, Cambridge CB2 8BS, United Kingdom

Cambridge University Press is part of the University of Cambridge.

It furthers the University's mission by disseminating knowledge in the pursuit of education, learning and research at the highest international levels of excellence.

www.cambridge.org
Information on this title: www.cambridge.org/9781107497580

© Cambridge University Press 1928

First published 1928
First paperback edition 2015

A catalogue record for this publication is available from the British Library

ISBN 978-1-107-49758-0 Paperback

PREFACE

Austin dobson, that wise and seasoned critic, said long ago that a new fact about Goldsmith had become a rarity, and all students who have examined the scanty biographical data concerning Goldsmith's life know this to be true. For this reason I have felt constrained, in assembling Goldsmith's correspondence, to include even fragmentary letters, and notes of negligible literary value, since all of them shed some light on the obscure history of his life. The bulk of the correspondence, however, needs no historical justification for its publication. It is singularly of a piece with the best of Goldsmith's prose.

The plan of this volume requires a word of explanation. Instead of beginning with the usual critical or biographical commentary, I have grouped in the Introduction a number of topics illustrating the letters, which seemed either too long for insertion in the footnotes, or too important (because of the new material which they embody) to be reduced to the limits of mere annotation. The topics thus treated are Goldsmith's relations with his family, the authenticity of his Fiddleback adventure, the abandonment of his East India voyage, the writing of *Threnodia Augustalis*, and the production of *She Stoops to Conquer*. The text of Mrs Hodson's memoir of her brother's early life, which forms one of the appendices, is here printed in its original state for the first time. It is included both because of its bearing on the authenticity of the letter to Mrs Goldsmith, and because of its intrinsic importance. The forged letters in the second appendix are included merely to safeguard future students of the letters from imposition.

I am indebted, in the preparation of this volume, to all the owners of Goldsmith's letters who generously permitted me to reproduce their MSS., and particularly to Miss Constance Meade, for placing at my disposal her unique Goldsmith collection. I wish also to thank the American Association of University Women, which aided me materially with a fellowship while the work on this book was in progress. My greatest debt of gratitude is to Professor Chauncey B. Tinker for his illuminating help and generous encouragement. His contribution to this volume is too diverse to be described.

K. C. B.

CONTENTS

INTRODUCTION

§ 1. GOLDSMITH AND HIS FAMILY

GOLDSMITH's letters, after he left Ireland in 1752, were filled with reminiscent tenderness. He complained of being forgotten, he begged for news, he recalled Lishoy fireside with fond regret, and laid plans for a happy return when his fortunes should permit. His works, too, are full of tributes to what seems a family relationship of the most ideal order—the dedication of the *Traveller* to his brother Henry, the portrait of his father as the Village Preacher, the implied reminiscences in the chronicles of the unforgettable Primroses. It is small wonder that all these have so charmed Goldsmith's biographers, and his readers, that they have allowed the more prosaic realities of his family history to pass for the most part unregarded. It seems only an act of belated biographical justice to piece together here as many of the less familiar facts of that history as can be gained from the surviving correspondence.

His father, his brother Henry, his uncle Contarine, and his brother-in-law Hodson, who were men of education and independent character, commanded his unquestioned love and esteem, and of them I have little to say here, since the representation of Goldsmith's feeling for them seems to be faithful enough in the biographies. One must not suppose, however, that Dr Primrose or the Village Preacher is in every detail a faithful portrait of the elder Goldsmith. If one turns to the story[1] told by Mrs Hodson of Oliver's boyhood, in which her father is represented as supplying the encouragement for the little boy's writing his indecorous verses, one feels at once the difference between the coarse Irish reality of the 1730's, and Goldsmith's refined and idealized memories, shadowed forth in his literary creations. But for his mother, his sisters, and his two younger brothers, between whom and the other members of the family there seems to have been considerable disparity in intellect and character, he apparently felt only a nominal family affection which weakened with separation.

Of his sisters we know little. Jane married beneath her, and was merely "poor Jenny." Catherine had a fair wit, and a turn for sprightly story-telling, as her account of her brother's boyhood shows; but although they were, as Maurice wrote to Bishop Percy, "both inseparable Companions in their youth," there was nothing strong enough in her to bind her brother's affections, and his

---

1 See Appendix III. Mrs Hodson's narrative also makes clear that the Man in Black's father was intended for the elder Goldsmith, not the Man in Black himself, as Percy mistakenly reported in the Memoir. The Man in Black is presumably Goldsmith himself.

letters are addressed to her husband, not to her. The mother was frugal and hard, and apparently quite unable to understand the improvident genius she had borne. There was an honest downright-ness about her, however, which commands respect. According to Mrs Hodson's narrative[1], when Oliver came home with his fine tale about his adventures at Cork, she gave him "many cool repremands," and, when he confessed that he had not written to thank the good counsellor, she called him "an ungratefull savage, a monster in short." Her exasperation hardened into an estrangement which even Goldsmith's biographers have not been able to overlook, and which apparently lasted through her life. His allusions to her in the sur-viving letters show at first a tone of jaunty bitter-ness. Writing to his cousin, Bob Bryanton[2], more than a year after he had left home, he attributed his previous neglect of writing to "an hereditary indolence" which, he said, he had from his mother's side—a veiled allusion, perhaps, to his mother's failure to write to him. He added in a flippant postscript: "Give My service to My Mother if you [see her] for as you express it in Ireland I have a sneaking kindness for her still." A second allu-sion to his mother, in a letter to his brother Hodson[3], written five years later, confirms the suspicion that she refused to write to him—"Pray let me hear from my Mother since she will not gratify me herself

1 See p. 171.   2 See p. 9.   3 See p. 55.

and tell me if in anything I can be immediately servicable to her." His tone in these later letters became dutiful, and even solicitous, but never affectionate, and when he received news of his mother's near-blindness, he used it capriciously as a reason for not coming home. "To behold her in distress," he said, "without a capacity of relieving her from it would be too much to add to my present splenetic habit."[1] He had earlier mentioned[2] his distress at the loss of her Pallas property and his inability to give her financial aid, and this, with one more request for news of her, in his letter to Maurice[3], in 1770, is the sum of the allusions to her. Miss Frances Reynolds told a story, which has been indignantly repudiated by Forster, that at his mother's death, in the summer of 1770, Goldsmith wore half-mourning only, and said it was for a distant relative. In the light of the circumstances the story does not seem impossible. "A distant relative" is no bad description of a mother from whom one has been separated and estranged for nearly twenty years.

After he left Ireland another estrangement occurred, between him and his cousin, Jane Contarine Lawder[4], although she had been, in Mrs

1 See p. 62.   2 See p. 32.   3 See p. 87.
4 Goldsmith's biographers have cherished a sentimental tradition that he had loved his cousin Jenny in his youth, but according to Michael F. Cox (*National Literary Society of Ireland's Journal*, I, pt 2, p. 81) Jane was married in 1735, when Goldsmith was

xii

Hodson's phrase, "verry fond of him and a particular Friend." The reason for it is not altogether plain, but it evidently arose at the time when Jane's father, Goldsmith's generous benefactor, lapsed into imbecility. This event, which Goldsmith wrongly recorded as his uncle's death[1] in the Memorandum of his life which he dictated to Percy, occurred while Goldsmith was in Padua, and obliged him, as he said, "to return back thro France &c on Foot." The indication is clear that he was still depending on his uncle for funds, in spite of his having told him[2] that he drew on him for his last twenty pounds before he left Edinburgh. After the event, Goldsmith did not write to his cousin Jane because, as he later told her, he was afraid his letters "might be regarded as the petitions of a beggar and not the offerings of a friend."[3] In other words, he did not write because he feared that the Lawders would interpret his letter as a request that they continue his uncle's bounty toward him. This silence of his, misinterpreted by the Lawders as a token of indifference, may well have been the cause of the coolness which they ever afterwards displayed toward him. Gold

probably only four or five years old. The attachment could hardly have been of a romantic character.

1 His uncle was still alive in August, 1758, when Goldsmith mentioned him in a letter to Jane Lawder. Cox, in the article quoted, says that the uncle died in 1758, in his seventy-fourth year.

2 See p. 16.   3 See pp. 42–3.

smith was genuinely distressed by it, and made repeated unsuccessful efforts at reconciliation. He commissioned Charles, who paid him a visit in 1757, to send him the particulars of their feelings for him[1]. Again, in 1758, he made inquiries of his sister Catherine about them, and, apparently at his sister's suggestion[2], wrote a conciliatory letter to Jane in August of that year. The Lawders did not respond, nor did they trouble to notify him of a legacy left him by Mr Contarine at his death. Goldsmith learned of it twelve years later, through his brother Maurice; and the last mention of the Lawders occurs in his reply to Maurice, in which he expresses his gratitude to them for their kindness "to our poor shattered family"[3] and mentions the fact that he is sending to Jane a miniature of himself—"tho' they have almost forgot me." Though he remained forgotten to the last, the honours for kindliness and right feeling were his.

Although Goldsmith preferred not to inform the Lawders of his destitution at Padua, he did make known the fact to his own family, and Dan Hodson levied a contribution on all his friends to help him. The money failed to reach him, nor did he know of the attempt until Charles told him of it in London. He wrote to Dan Hodson[4] that his not receiving that sum was responsible for his settling in London; its miscarriage thus formed an important turning-point in his career.

1 See p. 53.   2 See p. 53.   3 See p. 85.   4 See p. 27.

xiv

Goldsmith did not, as a matter of fact, ever again return to Ireland, although he reiterated his intention of doing so even as late as 1771, in the last surviving family letter[1]. The sincerity of his professions may be questioned here, although Goldsmith himself probably hardly realized that the successive postponements of his visit to Ireland were good-natured but specious disguises of a waning interest. After his prosperity began, he certainly often commanded both time and money sufficient to make the journey, if he had wished. In the summer of his mother's death, he was abroad on a journey to France with the Hornecks, which might well have been, had he desired, a journey to Ireland.

After his establishment in London he kept, however, in closer touch with his family than has generally been supposed, through the visits which his two younger brothers paid to him. Charles and Maurice, as yet unsettled in the world, and not having ambition or education enough to rise by their own efforts, turned to their gifted brother with hopes of advancement as soon as they heard of his first small success in London. Charles, being the more enterprising, actually sought his brother out in London, late in 1757, arriving penniless and without prospects. Goldsmith himself was not much better off at the time. He had given up his "thraldom" under Griffiths as reviewer for the

1 See p. 102.

Monthly Review in August, and had no regular employment, but was living precariously by hack-work, such as translating *The Memoirs of a Protestant*. Under the circumstances, he did not welcome the arrival of Charles, and as soon as he could he packed him back again to Ireland. Goldsmith's letter to Dan Hodson[1] on December 27 speaks of Charles' visit, and of his impending return, pro-vided with "everything necessary," and he adds a hope that he will be "improved...against his return." The worn passages in the text of the letter unfortunately leave tantalizing gaps in our under-standing of what improvements Oliver desired in his brother, or of the connection in which the "stranger" assisted him. In another letter[2] to the Hodsons eight months later Goldsmith alludes a second time to Charles, again in a badly worn passage. The legible portion makes clear that he either had settled at home to some business or was being urged to do so by his family. The busi-ness he took up was probably the trade of cabinet making[3].

We know nothing more of Charles until twelve years later, when his restless mood again overtook him, and he departed to Jamaica to seek his fortune, some time in the latter part of 1769, probably without telling his family of his destination. In an

1 See p. 31.   2 See p. 54.
3 That was the trade he followed later in Jamaica. See p. xviii.

ordinary family one would expect a prompt report of such a momentous event to go at once to distant members of the family circle. But not so with the Goldsmiths. No one troubled to inform Oliver in London that Charles had gone. He did not know of it until Maurice alluded indirectly to it in his letter of January, 1770, in calling himself Goldsmith's "only brother."[1] This puzzled the recipient completely, and when he answered Maurice's letter he asked him to explain—"You talk of being my only Brother. I don't understand you. Where is Charles?"[2] We do not know if Maurice answered his brother's inquiry, but we do know that reassurance about his brother's whereabouts and safety came shortly from a more satisfactory source, Charles himself. He wrote to Goldsmith some time before April or May of that year, telling him of his settlement in Jamaica, and Goldsmith passed the information on to Dan Hodson, without comment, as a postscript to more important matters: "I had a letter from Charles who is as he tells me possessed of a competency and settled in Jamaica."[3] The last surviving mention which Oliver made of Charles was in the Memorandum of his life which he dictated to Percy in April, 1773, in which he

[1] Maurice must of course have made clear that he meant "the only brother *left at home*," for Goldsmith so understood it. If he had supposed that Maurice was reporting his brother's death, he could not have added, "A sheet of paper occasionally filled with news of this kind would make me very happy."
[2] See p. 87.   [3] See p. 91.

xvii

duly mentions his brother as having gone to Jamaica as a cabinet maker "where he now lives possessed of a good fortune."[1]

This sums up all that we know of Goldsmith's connection with his youngest brother. It is a very slight basis on which to determine the nature of Goldsmith's feelings for this brother, but the very slightness and coldness of the allusions show clearly that there was no close bond of affection between them. There is a decent brotherly interest in his welfare, and no more. The historical Charles, we feel certain, could have been only a remote original of either little Bill or little Dick, whose portraits Goldsmith drew with such indulgent tenderness in *The Vicar of Wakefield.*

Besides helping to discredit the autobiographical significance which readers have persisted in seeing in *The Vicar of Wakefield*, this account of Charles' movements serves also to bury a tradition about him which has been preserved by all Goldsmith's biographers. This tradition reported that Charles ran away to Jamaica in 1757, after Goldsmith received him coldly in London, and that he never afterwards communicated with his family, so that they did not know where he was, and came to look upon him as dead. This myth began with Northcote's doubtful second-hand account[2] of Charles'

1 See the writer's *History and Sources of Percy's Memoir of Goldsmith,* p. 14.
2 *Life of Sir Joshua Reynolds,* I, 331.

return to England in 1791, in which he is represented as saying that he had been "for many years
supposed to be no longer in the land of the living."
Northcote, who had seen the passage in Goldsmith's letter to Maurice, asking about Charles,
inferred that he was at that time supposed dead
by his family, and Forster, carrying the misinter-
pretation still further, drew the conclusion that
he had left for Jamaica in 1757, after being
repulsed by Oliver in London, and was not heard
from after that time. The inference that Charles
could have disappeared in 1757 and could have
been supposed dead by his family in Ireland for
thirteen years without their communicating the
fact to Goldsmith, who had been the last to see him,
seems too absurd to have gained credence under
any circumstances; and with the evidence afforded
by the recovered portions of the correspondence it
becomes definitely discredited.

Goldsmith's relations with his next younger
brother, Maurice, were no more satisfactory than
those with Charles. Two passages[1] in Goldsmith's
early letters to his family, from London, which
Maurice carefully crossed out before sending the
letters to Bishop Percy, in 1776, show that he, too,
contemplated a visit to his brother in London in
1757, and that he even suggested going on the
proposed voyage to India with him. Goldsmith
firmly discouraged this latter proposal, because of

[1] See p. 54, note 2, and p. 61, note 4.

xix

its cost, but he offered, with kind brotherliness, to secure him a position, evidently of a clerical sort, if Maurice would only improve in his writing and spelling. He warmly urged his coming, as a step to his ultimate betterment, and arranged to have his passage money sent him, to share his chamber in the Temple with him, and to give him some of his own clothes, if those necessities were lacking. He even promised to send back for his brother from India, if he prospered there. But apparently the conditions were too severe for Maurice to meet. Goldsmith made the proposal at the end of August, and by January Maurice had as yet sent him no "specimen of his perform-ance" to show to prospective employers. Judging by the one specimen of Maurice's letter-writing which survives among Bishop Percy's papers, he failed throughout his life to master the difficulties of spelling and grammar. This unwillingness, or inability, of Maurice's to help himself evidently alienated his brother's sympathy and interest. There is no record of their further connection until 1770, when Goldsmith wrote a kind letter[1], ex-pressing his willingness, but inability, to help the yet unsettled fellow, and signing over to him, in response to an evident hint, a legacy of fifteen pounds left him by his uncle. Maurice used the money to take a journey to London, which Gold-smith mentioned with wry brevity in a letter to

1 See p. 83.

Dan Hodson a few months later—"My brother
Maurice was with me in London but it was not in
my power to serve him effectually then; indeed in
a letter I wrote him I desired him by no means to
come up but he was probably fond of the journey."[1]
It was presumably on this occasion that Goldsmith
gave his brother the advice which Maurice reported
later to Percy, to learn the trade of cabinet making,
and to give up the idea of being a gentleman—
advice which it may be said to his credit that he
followed.

Goldsmith's statement that he was unable to
help his brother at this period must be taken with
reservations, and probably means that he did not
consider it expedient to encourage Maurice's
parasitical bent, and his shallow aspirations to
gentility. Certainly Goldsmith's literary fame was
at its height after the publication of *The Deserted
Village*, on May 26 of that year, and the income
from his writing in the months just preceding had
been great. His power of securing patronage, if
he had desired it, must have been considerable,
especially from his intimate friend and patron,
Lord Clare, of the old Westmeath Nugent family,
who was a lord of the treasury and vice-treasurer
of Ireland. Goldsmith carefully guarded knowledge of this friendship from his Irish connections,
knowing probably by experience what an effect
the glitter of that name would have upon them.

[1] See p. 91.

When he wrote to Dan Hodson in 1771[1] about his son William's situation, he had to allude to the circumstances which had called him out of London in April, but he refrained from saying that the dying friend with whom he had travelled to Bath was Lord Clare's only son, Colonel Nugent. What Goldsmith could do in the way of securing patronage and bestowing favours, when he thought them deserved, and when his own affections prompted, is seen in his treatment of his nephew William Hodson, who came to London shortly after Maurice, in the late spring or early summer of 1770[2], with an ambition to become an actor. Goldsmith energetically intervened, persuaded him to abandon the stage and instead to continue a medical training begun at Dublin, wrote to the great Dr Hunter[3] in his behalf, provided him with clothes and money, and wrote to his father urging him to help in the young man's support. In the next year, after Dan Hodson had refused to continue his son's support, Goldsmith secured for him, through the influence of a friend, probably Reynolds, "a place as full surgeon to India." At Goldsmith's death, the largest item on his unpaid

1 See p. 99.
2 The fact that William Hodson witnessed the legal transfer of the legacy money, which Maurice spent for his journey to London, suggests that they came together. (See p. 85, note 1.) Prior mistakenly placed this visit in 1766, and Forster supposed that there were two visits.
3 See p. 88.

tailor's bill was thirty-five pounds and three shillings, charged to Mr Hodson's order. This is the end of Maurice's story. At Goldsmith's unexpected death, in April, 1774, he hurried to London to administer his brother's estate, but, finding nothing but debts, was obliged to return empty-handed as he came. From that time until 1801 various members of the family lived in vain expectation of returns from Bishop Percy's benefit edition of the poet's works. The Goldsmiths were fated to gain no more profit or worldly consequence from their brother's fame after his death than they had during his life. Their only reward has been an immortality, which some of them did not deserve, as the originals of the idyllic family circle of the Primroses.

§ 2. THE ADVENTURE UPON FIDDLEBACK

The recovery of the original text[1] of Mrs Hodson's account of Goldsmith's early life makes possible a clearing up of some of the mystery attending upon Goldsmith's curious story of his adventure upon Fiddleback. The story, which was first published by Percy, is important, not only because it furnishes an early and striking example of Goldsmith's improvidence and his affinity for curious experiences, but more particularly, because it contains prophetic suggestions of the character of the Man

1 See Appendix III.

in Black, the adventures of Jack Spindle, and the
incident of the oak staff in *The Vicar of Wakefield*.
It raises the nice question whether Goldsmith
actually based his fictions on his experiences, or
whether the experiences were not themselves
fictions—the products of an already active imagination. Because of these singularities, the story,
although accepted by all the biographers, roused
doubt in many a reader from the first. Malone
thought that Mrs Hodson had made it up, and
told Percy so[1]. Scepticism seemed to be silenced,
at least concerning Mrs Hodson's veracity, when
Prior published the actual text of a letter[2] from
Goldsmith to his mother, which he believed him
to have written after his verbal account, in an
attempt to convince his mother of the truth of his
tale. "The original of this letter," Prior said, "is
not to be found; but a copy seems to have been
in the possession of Mrs Hodson, who communicated the material facts in the memoranda
furnished of the early portion of her brother's life.
It [the copy] is now in the possession of the gentleman who holds the original MS. memoir, and was
probably sent by her at a subsequent period."[3]
In view of the facts that neither Percy nor Malone

1 "Have you any faith in the story that his sister tells of...his
excursion to the county of Cork, where we have a long story
furnished by this lady without a single *name* or *date*?" (Prior, I,
126).
2 See p. 148.
3 Prior, I, 119.

was aware in 1802 of the existence of such a letter[1], and that Mrs Hodson had died before that date, the copy could only have reached Percy through one of Mrs Hodson's children; and the motive for sending it after that date, when the Memoir had already appeared, is hard to imagine. Other circumstances, which an examination of Mrs Hodson's original manuscript brings to light, make Prior's theory even more difficult to accept.

Mrs Hodson's account of the Fiddleback episode, from which Percy drew his own, but which no subsequent biographer has examined, corresponds so exactly with the account in Prior's letter that it is clear either that the letter was based on her narrative, or her narrative on the letter. Prior, of course, believed the latter. But in Mrs Hodson's account, the circumstances of the telling of the story are not ambiguous. She reports the story as from Goldsmith's own mouth, with a vivid description of the family scene which took place afterwards. Mrs Hodson knew very well the value of her brother's letters, and if there had actually been a letter to draw upon here, she would certainly have quoted it explicitly. One would have to suppose, in order to believe Prior, not only that she deliberately concealed the existence of the letter, but that she actually falsified the account to make it appear a verbal one. Furthermore, the conclusion of the story, which Percy omitted, and

[1] See Malone's and Percy's letters on the subject, Prior, I, 125–8.

xxv

which the letter, for obvious reasons, likewise omitted, makes the writing of any letter at all a patent absurdity. It reads:

And now Dr Mother says he since I have struggeld so hard to come home to you why are you not better pleas͏d to see me, and pray says the Mother have you ever wrote a letter of thanks to that dear good man since you came home, no says the Dr I have not then says the Mother you are an ungratefull Savage a Monster in short the whole boddy of his Freinds which ware present up braid͏d him for which he for a full half houre sat listning to with grate composure and after they had vented their Passion he beg͏d they wod sit down and compos themselv͏s for what he told them was only to amuse them and that there was not one word in it; how ever he afterward assur͏d me of its veracity.

The absurdity of supposing that Goldsmith went off and wrote a minute account of the adventure which he had already told at length, and which he had later declared before the whole family to be an invention of his own to amuse them, is obvious. Furthermore, the style of Mrs Hodson's narrative shows no evidence of being derived from the letter. Rather, the letter shows every evidence of being a polished and reconstructed version of her narrative. Mrs Hodson writes in a rambling, discursive fashion, with irrelevant, but natural intrusions, such as the sick friend's inquiry whether Goldsmith had then come from Dublin or his mother's; while the sentences in the letter are compressed, show a careful rearrangement and elimination,

xxvi

and are phrased with a jaunty sophistication which is not only entirely foreign to the style of Mrs Hodson's account but also to Goldsmith's own way of writing[1]. Phrases appear also which are stiff with a false kind of elegance of which Goldsmith was never guilty, and of which the narrative of Mrs Hodson is likewise entirely innocent, phrases such as "the city and its environs," "circumstances of vicinity," "abundance without profusion and elegance without affectation." In Mrs Hodson's narrative numbers are given exactly, i.e. the distance from Cork to Ballymahon was a hundred and twenty miles, Oliver borrowed three half guineas from his host, while in the supposed source the distance was "above an hundred," and Oliver saw fit to borrow only a guinea. The natural deduction, of course, from these facts, is that the version with the blurred details and round numbers is the derived version.

Since the letter's history is so obscure and difficult of acceptance, and since all the internal evidence militates against it, the only conclusion to be drawn is that Prior was deceived about the letter's authenticity, either by deliberate hoax, or by accident. The most plausible reconstruction of

[1] One of these phrases, "If you will *sit down* and calmly listen to what I say," corresponds to Mrs Hodson's, "he then told his mother if she cd. cooly sit down," but the remark, besides becoming more impudent when transferred to a letter, becomes pointless as well.

the circumstances which led to this deception would seem to be that some one who had access to the manuscript of Mrs Hodson's narrative deliberately constructed the letter on the basis of her account, from what motive of course is unascertainable, but probably as a *jeu d'esprit*. The most probable agent is Henry Boyd, Percy's last collaborator in the Memoir, who must certainly have had access to Percy's MSS. Boyd died in 1832, five years before Prior's *Life* appeared, and it is perfectly possible that when Prior saw the "copy" it had fallen into the hands of Boyd's heir, or some purchaser who really did not understand the nature of the document, and supposed in good faith that it was a genuine transcript of an early letter. Prior's own statement that the copy belonged to "the gentleman who holds the original MS. memoir" strengthens this theory, since the "original MS. memoir" to which he refers is the early version of Percy's Memoir written by Campbell, and corrected by Percy[1], which Percy later turned over to Boyd for re-writing, and which could easily, in the natural course of events, have remained in his hands, and been transferred with his other papers after his death.

On the more important aspect of the riddle of the Fiddleback story, the question of Goldsmith's veracity in the telling of it, the only new light which can be thrown is Goldsmith's own confession,

1 Prior, I, p. xiii.

reported in his sister's account, that "what he told them was only to amuse them and that there was not one word [of truth] in it." This is followed, to be sure, by the teasing contradiction that he "afterward assur^d me of its veracity," but the whole incident bears the aspect of a tale of a tub, which, ironically enough, overshot its mark, and brought down as much abuse upon him for his ingratitude as he had feared to incur for his improvidence, so that he had to repudiate his own fine tale. His later assurance to his sister may have been an attempt to save his face, or, possibly, may indicate that there was a kernel of truth mixed in with the fiction. Probably Mrs Hodson herself was responsible for many details in the story, relying as she did on a twenty-five-year-old memory of the events, and supplied, as she indubitably was, with a lively imagination of her own. But the central structure was clearly Goldsmith's own. It seems safe to conclude that the surprising story of Fiddle-back was Goldsmith's first fiction, and that the character of the Man in Black, the adventures of Jack Spindle, and the unforgettable incident of the oak staff, adapted from Bishop Jewell, had been already partially conceived by him before he left Ireland. If this be true, it serves as a forceful illustration of the slow germination of Goldsmith's ideas, and of his singularly frugal husbanding of his imaginative resources.

§3. GOLDSMITH'S EAST INDIA PLAN

Goldsmith's unexplained abandonment of his plan to go to the coast of Coromandel as a physician, which he formed in 1757, and actively cherished for nearly two years, has always been a mystery. The last mention of the plan in his correspondence is in his letter to Henry Goldsmith, written in the middle of January, 1759—"I have met with no disappointment with respect to my East India Voyage nor are my resolutions altered." But he did not go, nor has any later allusion to the plan survived. Prior, who discovered the record of Goldsmith's rejection as hospital mate to a man-of-war on December 21, 1758, supposed that lack of funds, or irresolution, had made him shift his ambition from a civil post to a military one, and that his rejection automatically disqualified him for the civil appointment he already held. In other words, he thought that Goldsmith was lying to Henry about his situation.

The real cause for the failure of the plan seems, however, not to have been under Goldsmith's control. A significant series of historical events which took place in India at this time, and which have been overlooked by Goldsmith's biographers, decided the matter for him. In April, 1758, French forces under Count Lally landed unexpectedly at Pondicherry on the coast of Coromandel with the declared intention of clearing the English from

their foot-holds, and re-establishing French supre-
macy in southern India. Lally captured Fort
St David and laid siege to Madras, the last English
stronghold on the coast. The siege was carried on
until February, 1759, when an English fleet
arrived, and forced the French to retire. The war
was continued along the coast, however, until
January, 1761, when the French surrendered at
Pondicherry, and left the English in control.

The news of Lally's attack in April, 1758, did
not reach the English public until the following
March. During the interval, on October 10 and
17, November 4, December 21, and January 13,
the *London Chronicle* published short bulletins from
India, all dated from the previous March, and
reporting India quiet. Then on March 22, 1759,
the news burst on England, from the Paris papers,
of the French successes. At that time, before news
of the English navy's success had arrived, Madras
seemed in imminent danger of falling, and England
about to be thrust out of southern India entirely.
The French papers accused the British East India
Company of having suppressed intelligence of the
French victories, which seems certainly to have
been the case, for the Company began sending
surreptitious aid to the beleaguered post in December. Eight men-of-war were fitted out, only
one of which was ostensibly destined for Fort
St George (Madras)[1], but all of which eventually

[1] See the *London Chronicle* for December 12, 1758.

arrived there, and participated in the relief of that post in February. On December 14, indeed, the *London Chronicle* went so far as to announce that a large body of troops was being despatched to protect the Company's settlements from the threat of French aggression, but there is no hint, in the carefully veiled wording of the announcement, that war was actually already precipitated with the French forces in India.

How these events affected Goldsmith can be conjectured in the main. The East India Company, having assigned a civilian physician to a post which, sometime in the summer of 1758, they learned they no longer controlled, and not wishing to make public the real state of affairs, probably simply postponed his sailing with evasions. Meanwhile, they were fitting out ships of war for Coromandel, and Goldsmith, seeing a chance to save the fifty pounds of his passage money, tried for a position as hospital mate on December 21, and failed. There is no reason to suppose that his failure cost him the civil appointment he had already secured. He seems only to have been waiting for the necessary funds from the sale of his *Enquiry into the Present State of Polite Learning* (which was published on April 2) to secure him civilian passage, when the news of March 22 revealed the true state of affairs in India. That of course destroyed his immediate prospects at once. And before the news of the lifting of the siege of Madras reached England, his book had appeared, his literary fortunes were looking up, and he was committed to trying his fate in London.

§ 4. THE *THRENODIA AUGUSTALIS*

For many years Goldsmith's authorship of the *Threnodia Augustalis*, performed in honour of the memory of the Princess Dowager on February 20, 1772, at Mrs Cornelys' Great Room in Soho, remained unknown. The fact escaped Percy, Malone, Steevens, Boswell, and all the others who helped to collect his works for the edition of 1801, and was only brought to light by Joseph Cradock, who helped Goldsmith with the music, and to whom Goldsmith gave a copy of the published piece. Cradock gave the book to Nichols the publisher, and through Nichols the piece appeared finally in Chalmers' edition of Goldsmith's works in 1810.

It is not hard to conjecture the reasons why Goldsmith concealed his connection with the piece. It has in itself little original merit, amounting to not much more than a compilation. And his services were engaged, not by any of the great Personages who were ultimately responsible for the affair, but by the humble William Woodfall, the printer, Mrs Cornelys' agent. Goldsmith was discharging no obligation of gratitude, as his biographers have hinted, but was turning an honest penny, in a none too distinguished manner. Amusing evidence of the imposing secrecy he employed is afforded by three letters[1] which Woodfall wrote to him in the course of the negotiation. The first one, dated February 10, 1772, reads:

W. Woodfall's Compliments to Dr. Goldsmith, his Proposal as to Price is agreed to. It was intended by W.W. to call on him this Morning to inform him that it was wished by Mrs. Cornelys to have the Entertainment consist of two Parts. Both with a view of relieving the Performers and preserving the Auditors from Dulness from too great a length of solemnity. As to the names of the Speakers, Singers, and Composers, they are as yet merely thought on to be procured. Mr. Lee and Mrs. Bellamy if they can be got. W.W. is to wait on Bach[2] this morning to know if he will undertake to adapt the Matter to Music already Composed, it being imagined by Mrs. C. that some of Handel and Purcel's Music is as proper for the occasion as any the at best new Composition, provided it can be so adapted without destroying its own Harmony and Effect. Dr. Goldsmith is himself, it is presumed, a Judge of Music, if any Proper Composition strikes him, his writing to it will be highly serviceable. The whole Matter is at present but an Idea; it is intended to perform *something* on the occasion of the Death of her late Royal Highness the P. Dowager; at present two speakers and three Voices with Chorus singers and a proper band are thought

---

1 In the collection of Miss Constance Meade, hitherto unpublished.
2 The "English Bach," son of John Sebastian Bach. As the next letter shows, he was not engaged. Mattio Vento was the composer finally selected.

necessary; if it appears to Dr. G. that more or less may be proper for the occasion, and his opinion does not occasion an Expence inadequate to the ultimate view of Profit on the side of Mrs. Cornelys, it will be adopted. Secrecy as to the name of the Author shall be inviolably preserved.

In bed. Monday Morning, Feb. 10, 1772.

Goldsmith got the piece together between Monday and Friday, in two parts, as suggested, and despatched it to Woodfall, evidently with the request that the composer should come to his chambers in Brick Court to discuss the musical adaptation. Woodfall's fawning reply reads:

Doctor Goldsmith,

I am so much afraid of failing in the Request I am about to make to you that I cannot come to speak but rather trust to the force of what I can say on Paper; However, your Reply will crown the Success or totally demolish the expected Effect of your Poem on the Princess Dowager. I have spent this day in an unwearied pursuit to ensure those Performers who were likely to add to the Consequence, which a representation ought to carry with it, if it bestow Reputation and Profit on its Author, its conductor, or any one concerned in it. I have engaged Mr. Lee and Mrs. Bellamy to speak it—Mrs. Baddeley and Mr. Champnes as two of the Singers; and Mr. Vento will set up all night to forward its Composition—The Difficulty is Mr. Vento most readily would come to you at any time but it is absolutely impossible to carry his Books, his instruments and the necessary Paraphernalia with him, he lies therefore under the indispensable Necessity of Desiring your Company for half an hour, his Chariot shall wait on you at any stated hour in the Morning; he declares it will be absolutely impossible for him (an Italian) to adapt the Music without inquiring your Sense and Meaning, and that he cannot possibly go on without seeing you this forenoon, but that every precaution shall be taken on his Side to ensure privacy and prevent your being known—as his request is founded upon such urgent necessity and as the whole matter is so materially important to me, I flatter myself you will on this occasion dispense with a Punctilio which in a Manner will not be violated altho it cannot be ceremoniously adhered to. No Man knows better what is due to Dr. Goldsmith's Merit and Consequence than I do, nor is there any Man more ready to make the proper sacrifice, but the present instance is from its nature so peculiar, so dependant on immediate attention that it is impossible to chalk out a middle Line of Conduct —Mr. Vento cannot continue without seeing you, where his instruments are at hand, but no other person will be present and I hope, you will be kind enough to comply. Another request equally important I have to make is, that if you see Mr. Vento you will on no account mention that Mrs. Cornelys is concerned in the Affair, particular and most cogent Reasons demand this Secrecy; the Story now stands that I am directed by some Persons of Consequence to procure the performance at some great Room in Westminster at the instance of several of the 1st Nobility, that the Room is not yet fixed on and that as soon as it is the Matter will be made public.

Considering you as a friend, I implicitly told you the real state of the Matter, but many very urgent Causes make it necessary that Mrs. Cornelys should not be known to act in it or have any Concern with it. I am Sir in eager Expectation of a satisfactory Answer On all occasions

Your very h^{ble} Servt

White Friars, Feb. 14, 1772.   W. WOODFALL

Woodfall was in a state of mind between his nobles and his poet, and the latter made it worse by postponing the interview with Signor Vento until Sunday. Meanwhile Goldsmith saw his friend Cradock, who was a musician of some skill, from whom he exacted a promise to attend a rehearsal of his performance on Sunday. A note from Woodfall, sent on Sunday morning, reminded him of his previous engagement with Signor Vento, and a hasty note had to be despatched to Cradock[1], apologizing, and postponing their appointment and the proposed rehearsal until Monday. Woodfall's note reads:

W. Woodfall's Compliments to Dr. Goldsmith, he shall think himself infinitely obliged to the Doctor for accompanying him this day. A Gentleman has lent him his Carriage and he will call on the Doctor by twelve or a Quarter after. When the Doctor has settled his Business with Vento, the Coach shall take the Doctor to the Temple or where he pleases.

White Friars. Feby 16, 1772.

And so we may leave the Doctor, going to his appointment in the "Gentleman's" coach, cloaked in dignity and secrecy.

1 See p. 107.

B   *c*

§ 5. THE PRODUCTION
OF *SHE STOOPS TO CONQUER*

After Colman had finally been, in Dr Johnson's phrase, "prevailed on...by much solicitation, nay, a kind of force," to produce *She Stoops to Conquer*, his objections to the "low" elements which the play contained still had to be overcome. We shall, of course, never know the full extent of the play's revision, or even the character of a great deal of detail that must have been pruned away; but some clear hints of matter excised may be found in one source of information hitherto overlooked by the play's historians. This source is the epilogue written for the play by Goldsmith's friend, Joseph Cradock of Gumley, which was printed in an abridged form with the play.

The unabridged version of this epilogue appears in Cradock's *Memoirs*[1], and is accompanied by a brief explanation of Cradock's connection with the play. In it he says that he had read the MS. of Goldsmith's play in Leicestershire, had altered it, and, in returning it, had sent the Address in the Character of Tony Lumpkin, which he describes as "a mere Jeu d'esprit...not intended to be spoken," and adds, "parts alluded to in it, had been even struck out by myself, as too free, in the Doctor's original manuscript." His boast of having altered the play has been ignored, or

[1] *Literary and Miscellaneous Memoirs*, London, 1826, I, 226.

quietly discredited, by Goldsmith's biographers. The epilogue does, however, furnish ample evidence of his having seen the play in its unpruned stage; and whether or not he was responsible for the later excisions is a matter which does not concern us here.

In the epilogue, Tony is represented as declaring his intention to go up to town with Bet Bouncer, "Turn Author, Actor, Statesman, Wit, or Beau, And stalk the Hero of the *Puppet Show*." His speech is ungrammatical, with "they admires," "they talks," and "it been't polite," and has an odd trick of adding an initial consonant to words beginning with a vowel, e.g. "n'only," and "Roratorio." In the play as we know it, neither of these traits appears. The impression of engaging loutishness is conveyed by more subtle means, and the play therefore gains definitely by the revision. Tony's company at the Three Jolly Pigeons is also shown by the epilogue to have included at least two characters, later omitted, who apparently impressed Joseph Cradock as more important than any of the others. The passage which refers to them, which was of course omitted in the version of the epilogue printed with the play, reads:

Bill Bullet now can drive a roaring trade,
And picks up Countesses in Masquerade,
Walks round the new Great-room with Dukes and
    Peers;
And swears he'll never balk his country jeers;

xxxix

Nay, more, they much admires his lounging gait,
And talks to him as to the Lords of State.—
And there's my Comrade too that lived o' th' hill,
Odzooks! he quite forgets his father's mill;
Says he was born to figure high in life,
And gets in keeping by a Nabob's wife.

Bill Bullet, who sounds as if he might have been
modelled on the gay bucks Goldsmith had known
in Westmeath in his youth, has disappeared entirely, and all that is left of the "Comrade that
lived o' the hill" is Tony's allusion, in Act 1,
Scene 2, to "the miller's gray mare."

From another source, this time an anonymous
letter[1] of criticism sent to Goldsmith after the first
night's performance, it appears that some small
verbal changes were made while the play was on
the boards, before it was printed. The letter reads:

Privy Garden.

If D. Goldsmith will listen to two or three criticisms
of several of his friends, present at his play last night,
they make no doubt but he may acknowledge them
just & make a few trifling alterations accordingly.

[1]   Mr. Quick rather overacts his part.
[2]   The Drunken servant that is called in by
      Marlow, is an unpleasing & surely an un-
      necessary character.
[3]   Tony says, I had rather leave a Hare in her
      form &c &c. Would not one of the similes be
      quite sufficient?

1 In the collection of Miss Constance Meade, as are the other
hitherto unpublished documents quoted in this account.

xl

[4]   Tony makes too many remarks on the illegibility of Hasting's letter: it tires.

[5]   Hardcastle taking his night's walk should be wrapt up in a cloak with the hood up. It is but natural: & will better account for Mrs. H.'s mistaking him for a robber.

[6]   The Audience should be made clearly to understand that the chaise is only stuck fast in the Horse pond & not overturn'd.

[7]   When Hardcastle directs his Servants how to behave; his calling for a glass of wine & their saying it is none of their places to fetch is foolish & has a bad effect.

[8]   After Mrs. Hardcastle has discovered the contents of Hasting's letter: that Gentleman enters almost instantly & reproaches Tony with it: when no one on earth can possibly guess how he (Hastings) should know that his letter has been seen by any one but Tony. Above all let the

[9]   Dullissimo Maccaroni be left out. That is much too low.

I am Yr. sincere friend & admirer.

Of these suggestions, the third, sixth, and eighth seem to have been approved by Goldsmith and acted upon. "I had rather leave a Hare in her form" does not appear in the play's text as we know it, but may have been the first version, or an adjunct, of Tony's speech at the end of the second act, "She has as many tricks as a hare in a thicket, or a colt the first day's breaking." Again, the situation of the travellers in the horse pond is clearly indicated by Hastings' interruption of Tony's narrative, "But no accident, I hope?" to

xli

which Tony replies, "No, no; only mother is confoundedly frightened," etc. And as for Hastings' discovery that his letter has been read by Mrs Hardcastle, it is made plausible, in a makeshift, theatrical sort of way, which suggests an eleventh-hour revision, by Hastings' speech as he enters, "So, sir, I find by my servant that you have shewn my letter, and betrayed us." It is, of course, possible that the anonymous critic misunderstood the dialogue at these points, but the nicely critical attention with which he was listening for possible flaws makes this seem improbable. Further revision after the play was on the boards is indicated by a criticism which appeared in the *Whitehall Evening Post* on the Thursday after the play's first performance:

Where he means to give a comic jest, he sometimes gives us a farcical one. We must remark however, that some of these redundancies were peculiar to the first representation, and were judiciously omitted the succeeding night.

The omitted witticisms may have been certain pieces of "stale ribaldry" purloined from Tom Brown, and certain second-hand jokes from Joe Miller, which a caustic critic accused him of using in the columns of the same paper on the preceding Tuesday.

Another obstacle which Goldsmith had to overcome at the last moment was the securing of a

xlii

suitable epilogue. His letter to Cradock[1] sketches the three abortive attempts made before one could be found to suit both Colman and Mrs Bulkley, the Kate Hardcastle of the play. The first one, from Arthur Murphy, was, as Goldsmith himself says, "more the outline of an Epilogue than an Epilogue." It was sent by Murphy in a letter written on March 2, from Aylesbury, "in the hurry of the Assizes." The letter itself has not come to light, but it is described by an old catalogue[2], in which it was once advertised for sale, as follows: "It expresses regret that he cannot keep his promise to write an Epilogue for Goldsmith's Comedy, but he sketches the salient points for Goldsmith's own use, and warns him not to consult Garrick about it or he will tell you *not to do it*, that he may hereafter make *use* of the hint for himself. If you adopt the scheme do it secretly." The plan had to be abandoned because it offended Mrs Bulkley.

Goldsmith then proceeded to make two unsuccessful attempts himself. The first, a quarrelling epilogue between Mrs Bulkley and Mrs Catley, was refused by Mrs Catley, and the second, for Mrs Bulkley alone, was condemned by Colman. Goldsmith turned over to Percy the MSS. of both these pieces in April, 1773, when the latter undertook the office of biographer for him, and Percy later published them in the 1801 edition, without

1 See p. 118.
2 W. E. Benjamin, *Catalogue of Autograph Letters*, March, 1886.

xliii

recognizing for what play they had been intended. The quarrelling epilogue, which was in Goldsmith's own hand, he printed verbatim, but the other, not in Goldsmith's hand, he altered freely. He transposed long passages, altered or omitted lines[1] which Goldsmith used over again in the fourth, accepted epilogue, and omitted one long passage which ridicules the content and the acting conventions of sentimental comedy. The original MS. is here printed in full, with the lines which Percy rejected italicized.

EPILOGUE—Mrs Bulkley

There is a place,—so Ariosto sings,
A Treasury for lost and missing things.
Lost human Wits have Places there Assign'd them,
And they who lose their Senses, there may find them,
But where's this place, this Storehouse of the Age?
The Moon, says he: but I affirm the Stage.
At least in many things I think I see
This lunar and our Mimic World agree
Both shine at night For but at Foote's alone
We scarce exhibit till the Sun goes down.
Both prone to change, no settled limits fix,
Tis said the folks of both are lunaticks.
But in this parallel my best pretence is
That mortals visit both to find their Senses.
To this strange spot Rakes, Macaronis, Cits,
Come thronging to collect their scattered Wits.
The gay Coquet, who ogles all the day,
Comes here by night, and goes a prude away.

---

1 Percy mentions these lines in his correspondence with Steevens concerning the Epilogue. See Nichols, *Illust.* VII, 24.

The Gamester too, who eager in pursuit
Makes but of all his fortunes one *va toute*[1],
Whose Mind is barren, and whose words are few;
"*I take the odds*"—"*Done, done, with you, and you,*"
Comes here to saunter, having made his betts,
Finds his lost senses out, and pays his Debts.
The Mohawk too—with angry phrases stor'd
As "damme Sir" and "Sir I wear a Sword:"
Here lesoned for awhile, and hence retreating,
Goes out, affronts his man, and takes a beating.
Here come the Sons of Scandal and of News
But find no Sense—for they had none to lose.
The poet too—comes hither to be wiser,
And so for once I'll be the Man's Adviser.
What could he hope in this lord loving Age,
Without a brace of lords upon the Stage,
In robes and stars, unless the bard adorn us,
You grow familiar, lose respect, and scorn us.
Then not one passion, fury, sentiment,
Sure his poetick fire is wholly spent!
Oh how I love to hear applauses shower
On my fix'd attitude of half an hour (*Stands in an Attitude*)
And then with whining, staring, struggling, slapping,
To force their feelings and provoke their clapping.
Hither the affected City Dame advancing
Who sighs for Opera's, and doats on dancing,
Who hums a favourite Air and spreading wide,
Swings round the room the Heinele of Cheapside[2],

1 Percy changed to read:

> The gamester, Too, whose wit's all high or low,
> Oft risks his fortune on one desperate throw.

2 Cf. the lines in the accepted epilogue:

> Doats upon dancing and in all her pride
> Swims round the room, the Heinel of Cheapside.

Taught by our Art her Ridicule to pause on
Quits the *Che faro*[1] and calls for Nancy Dawson.
Of all the tribe here wanting an Adviser
Our Author's the least likely to grow wiser,
Has he not seen how you your favours place
On Sentimental Queens, and Lords in lace;
Without a Star, a coronet or Garter,
How can the piece expect, or hope for Quarter.
No high-life scenes, no sentiment, the creature
Still stoops among the low to copy Nature.
Yes, he's far gone. And yet some pity mix
The English Laws forbid to punish Lunaticks.

This epilogue not meeting with favour from Colman, Goldsmith was obliged to try a third time, and probably as late as Sunday afternoon or evening, March 14[2], the day before the first performance was given, he sent the resulting "mawkish thing" to Younger, the Covent Garden stage manager. Along with the epilogue, he sent Younger an additional title, also an eleventh-hour inspiration, to be added to the bills. Younger's answer, still surviving, reads:

Mr. Younger's Compts. to Doctor Goldsmith he recev'ed his note & has ordered the Bills to be alter'd

---

1 Changed by Percy to "*ballet*" probably because of the line's close resemblance to the line in the accepted epilogue:

And quits her Nancy Dawson for *Che Faro*.

2 Prior knew that the title was fixed on very near to the date of the first performance, but erroneously supposed the interval to be three days.

as he desires—Mrs. Bulkley has got a fair Copy of the Epilogue & he will take care in the Morning that the Licenser shall have another, & also the additional Title to the Play, & most sincerely wishes the Doctor Success.

Sunday Evening.

The "additional title" was, of course, "She Stoops to Conquer." Up to the moment, no better name had been found than "The Mistakes of a Night," although, as we know from Dr Johnson, all Goldsmith's friends had been "in labour" for a better one. It is probable that the original suggestion for this most appropriate and happy title came from Goldsmith's own line in the rejected epilogue:

...the creature,
Still stoops among the low to copy nature.

Certainly, the rejected epilogue had been in the fore-front of his mind while he composed the last one, since, as we have seen, he salvaged as many lines from it for his new effort as could be conveniently adapted. And since the last epilogue and the new title seem to have been conceived simultaneously, it is plausible to suppose that the title occurred to him while he was considering how he could utilize the suggestion of the line under consideration—a line which expressed more neatly than any other the play's intention, as its author saw it. "Stoops to copy" might easily have suggested

xlvii

"Stoops to Conquer," and the trick would have been turned[1].

Mrs Bulkley had learned the new epilogue by the next morning, and sent to Goldsmith to request that he hear her speak it. Her neat little note to him was among the papers which he later turned over to Percy:

> Mrs. Bulkley presents Compt^s to Dr. Goldsmith, shall esteem it a favour if he will take the trouble of calling on her this Morn^g as soon as convenient; she being perfect in the Epilogue, & very desirous of the Doctor's hearing it.
>
> Monday Morn^g

This final epilogue seems to have sprung from a suggestion in the rejected offering of Cradock, referred to above. In Cradock's piece, Tony and Bet Bouncer are represented as going to town and exchanging their country manners for the affectations of London. In Goldsmith's, Kate Hardcastle, still posing as the barmaid, does it instead. The device here is a poor thing, since it has no connection with the real character of Kate Hardcastle, nor with the point of the play. Goldsmith's own characterization of the epilogue as mawkish is just.

Of the success of the play, nothing need be said. Its disappointment of Colman's fears became, as

---

1 This does not, of course, preclude the possibility that the final phrasing may have been crystallized, as Mitford thought, by Dryden's line,

But kneels to conquer, and but stoops to rise.

xlviii

every one knows, a *cause célèbre*, and offered matter for numerous squibs at Colman's expense in the daily papers. On March 23 Goldsmith paid Colman a visit, to discuss the play's impending publication, at which time Goldsmith seems to have declared, in not too gracious a manner, his intention of mentioning Colman's opposition in the preface. That night, left on tenterhooks, and tried past endurance, Colman wrote Goldsmith a supplicating letter, which the latter was not above showing, or at least quoting, to Dr Johnson, who in turn, on March 25, passed the tid-bit on in a letter to Mrs Thrale[1]. The actual text of Colman's letter is at last available:

Tuesday night, Just going to bed.

Dear Goldsmith　　　　　　　(March 23 1773)[2]

Let me beseech you to put me out of my pain one way or other. Either take me off the rack of the Newspapers, or give me the *Coup de Grace*. In a word, & without a figure, I beg if you think I was vile enough to *wish* ill to your play (whatever I thought of it) e'en say so in yr. preface to it—but if you acquit me of this in your own mind, absolve me in the face of the World. In the latter case, you owe me this justice, for you have occasioned me to be loaded with abuse, insomuch that had I been yr. most inveterate enemy, or had you been so to me, I cd. not have been treated otherwise. All this has been owing to a frankness and candour wch. I cd. never have exercised in so great

1 Piozzi, *Letters of Dr Johnson*, 1, 80.
2 The date is added in a different hand.

a degree but to a friend. But enough of this; for I shall only repeat what I have said before, & what I have urged to you personally.

I forgot to tell you this morning, that it is unusual to publish a play till at least the Author's second Benefit is over. And keeping it out of print certainly keeps Curiosity alive & tends to serve the houses— I think therefore that practice is best, but do as you think best—indeed I sh⸢ not venture to advise.

Yrs.

G. COLMAN

Goldsmith did not see fit to comply with Colman's suggestion that publication be deferred until after the second benefit performance, on April 12, but brought the play out three days after the interview, on March 26. But the genuine distress which the letter exhibited, as well, probably, as the evident justice of Colman's complaint, led Goldsmith to give up any intentions he may have had of exulting over his discomfited friend in his preface. This preface, which took the form of a dedicatory letter to Dr Johnson, the play's staunch friend and most discerning critic, did indeed allude to Colman's doubts of the play's success, but in such temperate and general terms that Colman himself could hardly have taken offence at them:

I have, particularly, reason to thank you for your partiality to this performance. The undertaking a comedy, not merely sentimental, was very dangerous; and Mr. Colman, who saw the piece in its various stages, always thought so. However, I ventured to

1

trust it to the public; and, though it was necessarily delayed till late in the season, I have every reason to be grateful.

Goldsmith's triumph had been great enough.

§6. THE TEXT

In every case where the MS. of a letter has been available for examination, the original text has been reproduced exactly, even to the spelling and punctuation. Exception was made, however, in the punctuation of four of the early letters (i, ii, iv, and vi), in which Goldsmith either ran his sentences together with no divisions, or used commas in place of periods. In these letters a sufficient number of sentence divisions have been introduced, or substituted for Goldsmith's original commas, to make the sense intelligible[1]. In the letters which Goldsmith wrote after settling in London, in which, whatever their faults of punctuation, the sense is always clear, no changes at all have been made. Letters based on a printed source reproduce that source exactly.

Percy's Memoir, frequently mentioned in the notes, appeared in volume one of *Goldsmith's Works*, published by the United Booksellers of London, in 1801. References to Prior's *Life of Goldsmith* are to the single edition of that work, in two volumes, London, John Murray, 1837.

[1] The punctuation of Letter iii, which is based on a MS. copy of the original, is corrected in the same way.

li

THE LETTERS

I

To DANIEL HODSON[1]

[Edinburgh, the winter of 1752–3][2]

....ance, This country has little or nothin[g which I can] give an account of so instead of a D[escription of the] country you must be contented with [an account of the] manner in which I spend my Time, [during the] day I am obligd to attend the Publick L[ectures. At night] I am in my Lodging. I have hardly an[y other s]ociety but a Folio book a skeleton my cat and my meagre landlady. I pay 22 Lb[3] per am for Diet washing and Lodging being the cheapest that is to be got in Edinburgh all things here being much dearer than in Ireland as money is made more Plenty by the Last Rebellion[4]. I read hard which is a thing I never could do when the study was displeasing. I have..........to three Professors, and bought som[e]......value of about three more which I w[as]......obligd to

1 From the original in the Huntington Library, never before published entire. The MS. is a fragment, badly torn. Missing passages have been conjecturally supplied in brackets whenever the context suggested them.
2 Goldsmith entered the medical school at Edinburgh in October, 1752. This is evidently his first letter to his brother-in-law.
3 A large amount. Dr Johnson points out, in the *Journey to the Western Islands*, 1775, that board and room for seven months at St Andrews cost from £10 to £15.
4 The Jacobite Rebellion of 1745.

buy, besides some cloath[s]¹....My Dr Dan my
Freinds sent four guin[eas]....but as I have been
promisd fifteen......by my Freinds Exclusive of
my Un[cle]²..........drawn on Mr Constable
for ten poun[ds]..........................
[genero]usly contributed to make mine happy.
...My Dᴿ Brotherᴿ your afftᵗ Freind

OLIVER GOLDSMITH

P.S. ....[e]very Freind as...particularly mentiond Each, there is one³ on whom I never think
without affliction but conceal it from him.
Direct to me at Surgeon Sinclairs in the Trunk
Close⁴ Edinburgh.

1 A tailor's account, beginning on January 24, 1753, is still preserved in the library of the University of Edinburgh. It reads,
"Two and one half yards of rich sky Blew sattin, one and one-
half yards of white Allapeen," etc.
2 His uncle Contarine, as the next letter shows, furnished him with
£10 a year. He seems to have relied, then, on receiving £25
a year for his expenses. According to Mrs Hodson's statement
(Prior, *Life*, I, 133), she and Henry Goldsmith shared his support with Mr Contarine.
3 Probably Jack Goldsmith, his youngest brother, born in 1740,
who, according to a story told by Prior (*Life*, I, 9, note), received
an injury on a long horse-back ride with his mother which "cost
her the life of her son." Goldsmith himself told Percy, in the
Memorandum of his life which he dictated in 1773, that this
brother died at about the age of twelve. He was still alive at the
close of 1753 (see Letter V), but must have died shortly after
that.
4 A short street in the heart of old Edinburgh, running between
High Street and the open place surrounding the old Physic
Garden.

4

II

To the Reverend THOMAS CONTARINE[1]

My Dʳ Uncle   [Edinburgh] May 8th 1753[2]

In your letter (the only one I receivd from Kilmore) you call me the Philosopher who carries all his goods about him yet how can Such a character fit me who have left behind in Ireland Every thing I think worth posessing freinds that I love and a society that pleasd while it instructed, who but must regret the Loss of such Enjoyments who but must regret his abscence from Kilmore that Ever knew it as I did, here as recluse as the Turkish Spy at Parris[3] I am almost unknown to Every body Except some few who attend the Proffesors of Physick as I do, apropos I shall give you the Professors names and as far as occurs to me their characters and first as most Deserving Mr Monro[4] Professor of anatomy. This man has broght the

1 From the original in the collection of Mr Oliver R. Barrett. It is addressed, "To the Revd. Mr. Thos. Contarine at Kilmore near Carick on Shannon in Ireland. Via London." It was first published by Prior, in his *Life*, in 1837.

2 This date, with the class books of Monro, fixes the beginning of Goldsmith's Edinburgh days at the opening of the autumn term in 1752.

3 Marana's *L'Espion Turc*, 1684, was translated into English by Bradshaw in 1687–93, as *The Turkish Spy*. It probably furnished the first hint for *The Citizen of the World*.

4 Alexander Monro, *primus* (1697–1767), first professor of anatomy at Edinburgh, and the founder of the medical school. His annual lectures lasted from October to May.

5

science he Teaches to as much perfection as it is
capable of and not content with barely Teaching
anatomy he launches out into all the branches of
Physick where all his remarks are new and usefull.
Tis he I may venture to say that draws hither such
a number of stu[dents] from most parts of the
world Even from Russia, he is [not] [1] only a skilfull
Physician but an able Orator and delivers things
in the[ir] nature abstruse in so Easy a ma[n]ner
that the most unlearn'd may, must understand
him, Plumer [2] Professor of chymistry understands
his busines well but delivers himself so ill that He
is but little regarded, Alston [3] Professor of Materia
medica speaks much but little to the purpose, the
Professors of Theory and Practice say nothing but
what we may find in the books laid before us and
speak that in so droneing and heavy a manner that
their hearers are not many degrees in a better
state than their Patients. You see then D^r S^r
that monro is the only great man among them
so that I intend to hear him another winter and
go then to hear Albinus [4] the great Professor at

1 The bracketed portions are worn away in the MS. and are
  supplied from Prior's text.
2 Andrew Plummer (1726–55), lecturer in chemical pharmacy.
3 Charles Alston (1683–1760), first professor of botany and
  materia medica at Edinburgh.
4 Bernard-Siegfried Albinus (1697–1770), son of the equally
  famous Bernard Albinus, and professor of anatomy at Leyden.
  He was a pioneer in the study of the mechanical structure of the
  skeletal and muscular systems.

Leyden[1]. I read a science the most Pleasing in nature so that my labours are but a relaxation and I may Truly say the only thing here that gives me Pleasure. How I enjoy the Pleasing hope of returning with skill and to find my Freinds stand in no need of my assistance. How many happy years do I wish you, and nothing but want of health can take from your happynes since you so well Pursue the paths that conduct to Virtue. I am My Dr Uncle your most oblig^d.

most affectionate Nephew

OLIVER GOLDSMITH

P S I draw this time for Six pounds and will draw next october but for four as I was obligd to buy Every thing since I came to Scotland Shirts not Even Excepted. I am a little more early the first year than I shall be for the future for I absolutely will not Trouble you before the Time herafter.

My Best love attend M^r and Mrs Lawder[2] and heaven preserve them. I am again   your Dutifull nephew   OG

I have been a month in the Higlands[3]. I set out the first day on foot but an ill naturd corn

---

1 All Goldsmith's professors had been educated at Leyden under Boërhaave, during whose regime it rose to be the first medical centre of Europe. It had declined in importance since his death in 1732.

2 His cousin, Jane Contarine, and her husband. For a discussion of his relations with the Lawders see § 1 of the Introduction.

3 *Sic.*

7

I have got on my Toe has for the future prevented
that cheap method of Travelling so the second day
I hired a horse of about the size of a ram and he
walkd away (Trot he could not) as pensive as his
master. In 3 days we reachd the Highlands. This
letter wod be too long if it containd the description
I intend giving of that country so shall make it the
subject of my next[1].

III

To ROBERT BRYANTON[2]

Edinburgh, Sepr. ye 26th 1753

My dear Bob

How many good excuses (and you know I was
ever good at an excuse) might I call up to vindicate
my past shamefull silence. I might tell how I wrote

1 The second postscript is added on a separate sheet of paper, of
coarser quality than the first. Apparently he had taken his
Highland holiday after writing the first part of the letter, and
this was added as explanation of the delay. The winter term
ended on May 1, and work in the summer term was optional.
2 From a contemporary copy of the original letter, sent to Percy
by Maurice Goldsmith, used in the Memoir, in 1801, and still
remaining in the possession of Percy's descendant, Miss Constance Meade. Prior also printed from a copy of the original,
then in the possession of the Rev. Thos. Handcock, of Dublin.
This version was chosen in preference to Prior's because the
latter is obviously carefully corrected, while this, though full
of mistakes evidently attributable to the copyist, such as the

a long letter at my first comeing hither, and seem
vastly angry at not receiveing an answer; or I might
alledge that business, (with business, you know
I was always pester'd) had never given me time to
finger a pen; but I supress these and twenty more,
equally plausible & as easily invented, since they
might all be attended with a slight inconvenience
of being known to be lies; let me then speak truth;
An hereditary indolence (I have it from the
Mothers side)[1] has hitherto prevented my writing
to you, and still prevents my writing at least
twenty five letters more, due to my friends in
Ireland—no turnspit gets up into his wheel with
more reluctance, than I sit down to write, yet no
dog ever loved the roast meat he turns, better than
I do him I now address; yet what shall I say now
I am enter'd? Shall I tire you with a description
of this unfruitfull country? where I must lead you
over their hills all brown with heath, or their
valleys scarce able to feed a rabbet? Man alone
seems to be the only creature who has arived to

use of the possessive form for plurals, is clearly an attempt at
a literal transcript.

The letter was much admired and copied. Wm Shaw Mason,
in his *Statistical Survey of Ireland* (III, 360), mentions a copy, believed to be the original, "preserved by the late Mrs. M'Dermott
of Ballymahon." It was published for the first time in the
Anthologia Hibernica in 1793.

Bryanton was Goldsmith's cousin, and they had attended
Trinity College at the same time.

1 An obvious sarcasm. See § 1 of the Introduction for an account
of Goldsmith's relations with his mother.

the naturall size in this poor soil; every part of the country presents the same dismall landscape, no grove nor brook lend their musick to cheer the stranger, or make the inhabitants forget their poverty; yet with all these disadvantages to call him down to humility, a scotchman is one of the proudest things alive. The poor have pride ever ready to releive them; if mankind shou'd happen to despise them, they are masters of their own admiration; and that they can plentifully bestow on themselves: from their pride and poverty as I take it results one advantage this country enjoys, namely the Gentlemen here are much better bred then among us; no such character here as our Fox-hunter; and they have expresed great surprize when I informed them that some men of a thousand pound a year in Ireland spend their whole lives in runing after a hare, drinking to be drunk, and geting every Girl with Child, that will let them; and truly if such a being, equiped in his hunting dress, came among a circle of scots Gentlemen, they wou'd behold him with the same astonishment that a Country man does King George on horseback; the men here have Gennerally high cheek bones, and are lean, and swarthy; fond of action; Danceing in particular: tho' now I have mention'd danceing, let me say something of their balls[1] which are very frequent here; when

1 This description of the Assembly ball has been used by Graham (*Social Life in Scotland in the Eighteenth Century*), and by Chambers

a stranger enters the danceing-hall he sees one
end of the room taken up by the Lady's, who sit
dismally in a Groupe by themselves. On the other
end stand their pensive partners, that are to be,
but no more intercourse between the sexes than
there is between two Countrys at war, the Ladies
indeed may ogle, and the Gentlemen sigh, but an
embargo is laid on any closer commerce; at length,
to interrupt hostility's, the Lady directeress or
intendant, or what you will pitches on a Gentleman and Lady to walk a minuet, which they
perform with a formality that aproaches despond-
ence, after five or six couple have thus walked the
Gauntlett, all stand up to country dance's, each
gentleman furnished with a partner from the
afforesaid Lady directress, so they dance much,
say nothing, and thus concludes our assembly;
I told a scotch Gentleman that such a profound
silence resembled the ancient procession of the
Roman Matrons in honour of Ceres and the
scotch Gentleman told me, (and faith I beleive
he was right) that I was a very great pedant for
my pains: now I am come to the Lady's and to
shew that I love scotland and every thing that
belongs to so charming a Country Il insist on it
and will give him leave to break my head that
deny's it that the scotch ladys are ten thousand

(*Traditions of Edinburgh*), to depict Edinburgh's social life at this
period. The Assembly, started in 1710, was patronized by the
Jacobite society of Edinburgh, and opposed by the Calvinists.

11

times finer and handsomer than the Irish. To be
sure now I see y^r Sisters Betty & Peggy vastly
surprized at my Partiality but tell y^m flatly I don't
value them or their fine skins or Eyes or good
sense or—a potatoe for I say it and and[1] will
maintain it and as a convinceing proof of (I am
in a very great passion) of what I assert the scotch
Ladies say it themselves, but to be less serious
where will you find a language so prettily become
a pretty mouth as the broad scotch and the women
here speak it in it's highest purity, for instance
teach one of the Young Lady's at home to pronounce the Whoar wull I gong with a beccomeing
wideness of mouth and I'll lay my life they'l
wound every hearer. We have no such character
here as a coquett but alass how many envious
prudes. Some days ago I walk'd into My Lord
Killcoubry's[2] don't be surpriz'd my Lord is but
a Glover, when the Dutchess of Hamilton[3] (that
fair who sacrificed her beauty to ambition and her
inward peace to a title and Gilt equipage) pass'd
by in her Chariot, her batter'd husband[4] or more
properly the Guardian of her charms sat beside

1 *Sic.*
2 William Maclellan, who at this time was merely claimant of the
title. His son established the claim in 1773.
3 The celebrated Elizabeth Gunning, one of the sensational
beauties of the period. She later became Duchess of Argyle.
For Goldsmith's later connection with the Duke and Duchess,
see the next letter.
4 The Duke was only twenty-nine.

her. Strait envy began in the shape of no less than
three Lady's who sat with me to find fault's in her
faultless form—for my part says the first I think
that I always thought that the dutchess has too
much of the red in her complexion, Madam I am
of your oppinion says the seccond and I think her
face has a palish cast too much on the delicate
order, and let me tell you adds the third Lady
whose mouth was puckerd up to the size of an
Issue that the Dutchess has fine lips but she wants
a mouth. At this every Lady drew up her mouth
as If going to pronounce the letter P. But how ill
my Bob does it become me to ridicule woman with
whom I have scarce any correspondence. There
are 'tis certain handsome women here and tis as
certain they have handsome men to keep them
company. An ugly and a poor man is society only
for himself and such society the world lets me
enjoy in great abundance. Fortune has given you
circumstance's and Nature a person to look
charming in the Eyes of the fair world nor do
I envy my Dear Bob such blessings while I may
sit down and [laugh at the wor]¹ld, and at myself
—the most ridiculous object in it. But [you see
I am grown downright] splenetick, and perhaps
the fitt may continue till I [receive an answ]er
to this. I know you cant send much news from
[Ballymahon, but] such as it is send it all every-

1 The bracketed portions, worn away in the MS., are supplied
from Prior's version.

13

thing you write will be agre[eable and enter-
tai]¹ning to me. Has George Conway put up a
signe yet ha[s John Bin]ley left off drinking
Drams; or Tom Allen g[ot a new wig?] But I
leave to your own choice what to write but [while
Noll Go]ldsmith lives know you have a Friend.

P.S. Give my sincerest regards not [merely my]¹
compliments (do you mind) to your agreeable
[family] and Give My service to My Mother if
you [see her] for as you express it in Ireland I have
a sneaking kindness for her still². Direct to me,
Student of Physick in Edinburgh.

IV

To the Reverend THOMAS CONTARINE³

[Edinburgh, c. December, 1753]⁴

My dear Uncle,

After having spent two winters in Edinburgh,
I now prepare to go to France the 10th of next

1 The emendation of the editor. Prior's version is incomplete at
  this point.
2 See § 1 of the Introduction.
3 From Prior's *Life*, where it was first published in 1837. The
  letter itself was lost sight of after 1904, when it was sold at the
  Ford sale, at Sotheby's. A portion of the text was reproduced,
  with evident fidelity, in the sales catalogue, and the variations
  between it and Prior's text are given in the notes.
4 The date is conjectural. Goldsmith evidently received the answer
  which he asked of his uncle (see Letter VI: "Sometime after

February. I have seen all that this country can exhibit in the medical way, and therefore intend to visit Paris, where the great Mr. Farhein[1], Petit[2], and Du Hammel de Monceau[3] instruct their pupils in all the branches of medicine. They speak French, and consequently I shall have much the advantage of most of my countrymen, as I am perfectly acquainted with that language, and few who leave Ireland are so.

Since I am upon so pleasing a topic as self applause, give me leave to say that the circle of science which I have run through, before I undertook the study of physic, is not only useful, but absolutely necessary to the making a skilful physician. Such sciences enlarge our understanding, and sharpen our sagacity; and what is a practitioner without both but an empiric, for never yet was a disorder found entirely the same in two patients. A quack, unable to distinguish the particularities in each disease, prescribes at a venture: if he finds such a disorder may be called

the receipt of your last"), and time must therefore be allowed for an exchange of letters between Edinburgh and Ireland, by way of London, before February 10, his sailing date.

1 Antoine F. Ferrein (1693–1769), professor of medicine and surgery in the Royal College in Paris from 1742 to 1768.

2 Antoine Petit (1718–94), who succeeded Ferrein in the chair of anatomy in 1768.

3 Henri-Louis Duhamel du Monceau (1700–82), celebrated botanist. The Sotheby catalogue version reads "Duhammel du Monson."

by the general name of fever for instance, he has
a set of remedies which he applies to cure it, nor
does he desist till his medicines are run out, or
his patient has lost his life[1]. But the skilful
physician distinguishes the symptoms, manures
the sterility of nature, or prunes her luxuriance;
nor does he depend so much on the efficacy of
medicines as on their proper application. I shall
spend this spring and summer in Paris, and the
beginning of next winter go to Leyden. The great
Albinus is still alive there, and 't will be proper
to go, though only to have it said that we have
studied in so famous an university.

As I shall not have another opportunity[2] of
receiving money from your bounty till my return
to Ireland, so I have drawn for the last sum that
I hope I shall ever trouble you for[3]; 't is 20 l.
And now, dear Sir, let me here acknowledge the
humility of the station in which you found me; let
me tell how I was despised[4] by most, and hateful
to myself. Poverty, hopeless poverty, was my lot,
and Melancholy[5] was beginning to make me her
own. When you—but I stop here, to inquire how

1 In Letters 24 and 68 of *The Citizen of the World* Goldsmith again
  ridicules quacks. It is ironic that he himself fell a victim to faith
  in Dr James' fever powders.
2 The Sotheby catalogue reads "opertunity".
3 See § 1 of the Introduction for an account of his uncle's further
  help to him.
4 The Sotheby catalogue reads "dispised".
5 The Sotheby catalogue reads "melancholly".

16

your health goes on? How does my cousin Jenny[1], and has she recovered her late complaint? How does my poor Jack Goldsmith? I fear his disorder is of such a nature as he won't easily recover. I wish, my dear Sir, you would make me happy by another letter before I go abroad, for there I shall hardly hear from you. I shall carry just 33 l. to France, with good store of clothes, shirts, &c. &c., and that with economy will serve.

I have spent more than a fortnight every second day at the Duke of Hamilton's, but it seems they like me more as a *jester* than as a companion; so I disdained so servile an employment; 't was unworthy my calling as a physician.

I have nothing new to add from this country; and I beg, dear Sir, you will excuse this letter, so filled with egotism. I wish you may be revenged on me, by sending an answer filled with nothing but an account of yourself.

I am, dear Uncle,

Your most devoted

OLIVER GOLDSMITH

Give my—how shall I express it? Give my earnest love to Mr. and Mrs. Lawder.

---

[1] See § 1 of the Introduction for an account of Goldsmith's relations with his cousin Jenny.

V

To ——————[1]

[Edinburgh, c. December, 1753][2]

..share of my native assurance I shew'd my Talent
and acquird the name of the facetious Irish man,
I have either dined [o]r sup'd at His Graces[3] this
fortnight every second day, as I did not pretend
to great things and let em into my circumstances
and manner of thinking very freely they have

1 From the original in the collection of Mr A. Edward Newton,
never before published. The MS. consists of the lower part of
a folio sheet, written on both sides, and evidently preserved for
the signature on the back. The recipient was probably Dan
Hodson. See Letter VII, note 3.

2 The date is conjectural. It must coincide with the date of the
preceding letter, to which he refers in the postscript.

3 Goldsmith's biographers have held various theories as to his
position in the household of the Duke of Hamilton. Forster
thought he might have been employed as a tutor, but in
view of the fact that the only child, James George Hamilton,
the future claimant in the famous Douglas case, was not born
until 1755, this seems improbable. Prior thought an acquaintance might have been formed on the strength of the Duchess'
Irish connections. This and the preceding letter, however,
indicate that he was patronized because of his reputation as an
entertainer. The fact that he dined with them makes fairly
certain that it is to this experience he alludes when he recounts
the experience of the Man in Black (*Citizen of the World*, Letter
27)—"I was admitted as flatterer to a great man. At first,
I was surprised that the situation of a flatterer at a great man's
table could be thought disagreeable...," etc.

recomended me to Mr Thos Coelehit.........
...............[al]ways sangun o[r perhaps
I should say] ambitious—adieu

OLIVER GOLDSMITH

I have wrote My Uncle Contarine a long letter[1]
relative to the above mentiond afair. I wish you
coud see it as it is much fuller than this.

VI

To the Reverend THOMAS CONTARINE[2]

Leyden [c. May 6, 1754][3]

Dᵣ Sᵣ

I suppose by this time I am accus'd of Either
neglect or ingratitude and my silence imputed to
my usual slowness of writing but believe me Sʳ
when I say that till now I had not an opertunity
of sitting down with that ease of mind, which
writing requird, you may see by the top of this
letter that I am at Leyden but of my Journey
hither you must be informd. Some time after
the receipt of your last I embarkd for Burdeaux

1 Evidently Letter ɪv.
2 From the original in the collection of Miss Constance Meade.
  It is addressed, "To the Revd. Mr. Thos. Contarine at Kilmore
  near Carrick on Shannon in Ireland." It was first published by
  Percy, in his Memoir, in 1801, with omissions which are noted
  below.
3 The date is supplied by the postmark, "MA 6".

on board a scotch ship calld the St Andrew, John Watt Master. The ship made a Tolerable apearance and as another inducement I was let to know that six agreeable passengers were to be my company, well we were but two days at sea when a storm drove us into a Citty of England call'd Newcastle upon Tyne. We all went a-shoar to refresh us after the fatigue of our voyage seven men and me. We were one day on shore and o[n th]¹e following e[ve]ning as we were all verry merry the room door bursts open enters a Serjeant and twelve Grenadiers with their bayonets screwd and put us all under the Kings arrest, it seems my company were Scotch men in the French service and had been in Scotland to enlist Soldiers for the French King. I endeavourd all I could to prove my inocence however I remain'd in prison with the rest a Fortnight and with difficulty got off even then, Dʳ Sʳ keep this all a secret or at least say it was for debt² for if it were once known at the

---

1 The bracketed portions are worn away in the MS. and are supplied from a contemporary copy, made by Mrs Hodson, in Miss Meade's collection.

2 The account of this episode given in Glover's *Life of Dr Goldsmith* (1774) states that Goldsmith was imprisoned in Sunderland for a debt contracted in Edinburgh for a fellow-student, and that he was "relieved...by the humanity of Dr. Sleigh and Mr. Lauchlan Macleane." This forms part of Dr Sleigh's reminiscences of Goldsmith, which Glover secured at first hand from that gentleman; and it therefore seems necessary to conclude either that Goldsmith deceived Dr Sleigh as to the cause of his arrest, or that he is here deceiving his uncle.

university I shoud hardly get a degree[1], but hear how providence interposd in my Favour. The ship was gone on to burdeaux before I got from prison and was wreckd at the mouth of the Graronne[2] and every one of the crew were drownd. It happen'd the last great storm. There was a ship at that time ready for Holland. I embarkd and in nine days thank My God arrivd safe at Rotterdam, from whence I Traveld by land to Leyden whence I now write.

You may Expect some account of this country and tho I am not as yet well qualified for such an undertaking, yet shall I endeavour to satisfie some part of your Expectations, nothing surprizes me more than the books every day publishd, descriptive of the manners of this country. Any young man who takes it into his head to publish his traveles visits the countries he intends to describe passes thro them with as much inattention as his valet de chambre and consequently not having a fund himself to fill a vollume he applies to those who wrote before him[3] and gives us the manners

1 This seems clear proof that there was no foundation for Goldsmith's statement to Percy, in the Memorandum of his life dictated in 1773, that he had secured the M.B. degree at Dublin "when he was about twenty." It does indicate, however, that it was Goldsmith's intention to continue working for his medical degree, with the hope of securing it upon his return.

2 *Sic.*

3 Goldsmith's own account has many striking similarities to the description of Holland given in Thomas Nugent's *The Grand Tour*, published in 1749.

of a country not as he must have seen them but
such as they might have been fifty years before,
the modern dutch man is quite a different creature
from him of former times, he in every thing
imitates a French man but in his easy disingagd
air which is the result of keeping polite company,
the dutch man is vastly ceremonious and is
perhaps exactly what a French man might have
been in the reign of Lewis the 14th. Such are the
better bred but the downright Hollander is one
of the oddest figures in Nature. Upon a head of
lank hair he wears a half cock'd Narrow leav'd
hat lacd with black ribon, no coat but seven
waistcoats and nine pairs of breeches so that his
hips reach almost up to his arm pits. This well
cloathd vegetable[1] is now fit to see company or
make love but what a pleasing creature is the
object of his apetite why she wears a large friez
cap with a deal of flanders lace and for every pair
of breeches he carries she puts on two petticoats,
is it not surprizing how things shoud ever come
close enough to make it a match. When I spoke
of love I was to be understood not in a—in short
I was not to be understood at all[2], a Dutch Lady
burns nothing about her Phlegmatick admirer
but his Tobacco. You must know Sʳ every woman
carries in her hand a Stove with coals in it which

1 He first wrote "man".
2 Percy omitted the passage "is it not surprizing...understood at
   all."

22

when she sits she sn[ug]s under her petticoats and
at this chimney Dozing Strephon lights his pipe.
I take it that this continuall smoaking is what
gives the man the ruddy healthfull complexion
he generally wears by draining his superfluous
moisture while the woman deprivd of this amusement overflows with such visciditys as teint the
complexion and gives that paleness of visage
which Low fenny grounds and moist air conspire
to cause. A dutch woman and a Scotch will well
bear an oposition. The one is pale & fat and the
other lean and ruddy. The one walks as if she
were stradling after a go cart and the other takes
too Masculine a stride. I shall not endeavour to
deprive either country of its share of beauty but
must say that of objects on this earth an English
farmers Daughter is most charming. Every woman
there is a complete beauty while the higher class
of women want many of the requisites to make
them even Tolerable.

Their pleasures here are very dull tho very
various. You may smoak you may doze: you may
go to the Italian comedy as good an amusement
as either of the former. This entertainment always
brings in Harlequin[1] who is generally a Magician
and in consequence of his Diabolicall art performs
a thousand Tricks on the rest of the persons of

1 Goldsmith's continued distaste for the character of Harlequin
is seen in the epilogue which he wrote for Lee Lewes, in the
character of Harlequin, in 1773.

the drama who are all fools. I have seen the pit
in a roar of laughter at his humour when with his
sword he Touches the glass another was drinking
from, 'twas not his face they laughd at for that
was maskd, they must have seen something vastly
queer in the wooden sword that neither I nor you
Sᵣ were you there cou'd see. In winter, when their
cannalls are frozen every house is forsaken and all
People are on the ice. Sleds drawn by horses and
skating are at that time the reigning amusements.
They have boats here that slide on the ice and are
driven by the winds. When they spread all their
sails they go more than a mile and an half a minite.
Their motion is so rapid that the Eye can scarce
accompany them. Their ordinary manner of
Travelling is very cheap and very convenient.
They sail in coverd boats drawn by horses and in
these you are sure to meet people of all nations.
Here the Dutch slumber the French chatter and
the English play cards, any man who likes company
may have them to his Taste. For my part I generally detachd myself from all society and was wholy
Taken up in observing the face of the country,
nothing can Equall its beauty. Wherever I turn
my Eye fine houses elegant gardens statues
grottoes vistas present themselvs but enter their
Towns and you are charmd beyond description.
No no[th]ing can be more clean [or beau]tifull.

Scotland and this country bear the highest
contrast. There Hills and rocks intercept every

prospect here tis all a continu'd plain there you might see a well dresd Dutchess issuing from a dirty close and here a dirty Dutch man inhabiting a Palace. The Sotch[1] may be compard to a Tulip planted in dung but I never see a dutch man in his own house, but I think of a magnificent Egyptian Temple dedicated to an ox.

Physick is by no means Taught here so well as in Edinburgh and [in] all Leyden there are but four British students[2] all nescsarys[1] being so extreamly Dear and the Professors so very Lazy (the chymicall Professor[3] excepted) that we dont much care to come hither. I am [no]t certain how long my stay here may be however I expect to [have] the happiness of seeing you at Kilmore if I [can next March.]

Direct to me if I am honourd with a letter from you to Madam De Allion's in Leyden. Thou Best of Men may heaven guard and preserve you and those you Love.

OLIVER GOLDSMITH

1 *Sic.*
2 Dr Ellis, one of these four, later supplied Percy with the anecdotes of Goldsmith's stay in Leyden which were included in the Memoir.
3 Jérôme-David Gaubius (1705–80), who succeeded Boërhaave as professor of chemistry at Leyden in 1729.

VII

To DANIEL HODSON[1]

Dear Sir

It may be four years since my last letters to Ireland, and to y[ou in partic]²ular[3]. I received no answer; probably because you never wrote [to me. My] Brother Charless[4], however, informs me of the fatigue you w[ere at in] soliciting a subscription[5] to assist me, not only among my [friends and relations,] but acquaintance in general. Tho' my pride might feel so[me repug]-nance at being thus relieved, yet my gratitude can

1 From the original in the collection of Miss Constance Meade. It is addressed, "To Daniel Hodson Esqr. at Lishoy near Ballymahon, Ireland." It was first published by Percy, in his Memoir, in 1801, with omissions which are noted below.

2 The bracketed portions are worn away in the MS. Percy's readings of these passages have in general been followed, except where they are obviously inaccurate. Corrections of such passages are noted.

3 The last letter to Hodson may be the fragment, Letter IV, con-jecturally dated December, 1753. He had certainly written to others of his Irish connections in the interval: witness the pre-ceding letter from Leyden, and Mrs Hodson's remark in her account of his early life that "he wrote several letters to his friends from Switzerland, Germany, and Italy." And in order to account for Charles' visit, we must assume some communica-tion with his own family since his settlement in London.

4 See § 1 of the Introduction for an account of Charles.

5 See § 1 of the Introduction for the probable explanation of this subscription.

26

suffer no [diminu]tion. How much am I obliged
to you, to them, for such generos[ity,] (or why
should not your virtues have the proper name) for
such charity to me at that Juncture. Sure I am
born to ill fortune to be so much a debtor and so
unable to repay! But to say no more of this; too
many professions of gratitude are often considered
as indirect petitions for future favours[1]; let me
only add, that my not receiving that supply was
the cause of my present establishment at London.
You may Easily imagine what difficulties I had
to encounter, left as I was without Friends,
recommendations, money, or impudence; and
that in a Co[untry] where my being born an
Irishman was sufficient to keep me [unem]ploy'd.
Manny in such circumstances would have had
recou[rse to] the Friar's cord, or suicide's halter.
But with all my fol[lies I] had principle to resist
the one, and resolution to com[bat the] other.

I suppose you desire to know my present
situation, a[nd since][2] there is nothing in it, at
which I should blush, or mankind [could censure,
I] see no reason for making it a secret; in short,
by a v[ery little] practice as a Physician and a
very little reputation a[s an author][3] I make a

1 Cf. Letter x, to Jane Lawder: "every acknowledgment for past
favours might be considered as an indirect request for future
ones."
2 Percy read "As" for "a[nd since]".
3 Percy read "as a poet"; "author" fits the lacuna better.

shift to live. Nothing more apt to introduce us to
the gates of the muses than Poverty; but it were
well if she only left us at the door; the mischief
is, she sometimes chooses to give her company
during the entertainment, and Want, instead of
being gentleman-usher, often turns master of the
Ceremonies. Thus upon hearing, I write, no doubt,
you immagine, I starve, and the name of an Author
naturally reminds you of a garret, in this particular
I do not think proper to undeceive my Friends;
but whether I eat or starve, live in a first floor
or four pair of stairs [   ] high, I still remember
them with ardour, nay my ve[ry coun]try comes
in for a share of my affection. Unaccountable
[fond]ness for country, this maladie du Pays, as
the french [call] it. Unaccountable, that he
should still have an affec[tion for] a place, who
never received when in it above civil [contem]pt[1],
who never brought out of it, except his brogue
[an]d his blunders; surely my affection is equally
ridiculous with the Scotchman's, who refused to
be cured of the itch, because it made him un-
co'thoughtful of his wife and bonny Inverary.
But not to be serious, let me ask myself what gives
me a wish to see Ireland again? The country is
a fine one perhaps? No!—There are good company
in Ireland? No; the conversation there is generally
made up of a smutty toast or a baudy song. The
vivacity supported by some humble cousin, who

1 Percy read "common civility" for "civil [contem]pt".

28

has just folly enough to earn his—dinner.—Then
perhaps ther's more wit and [lea]rning among
the Irish? Oh Lord! No! there has been more
[money] spent in the encouragement of the
Podareen mare[1] there [in on]e[2] season, than given
in rewards to learned men since [the ti]mes of
Usher[3]. All their productions in learning amount
[mayb]e[4] to, perhaps a translation, or a few
tracts in labo[rious[5] div]inity, and all their productions in wit, to just nothing at all. [Why the
p]lague then so fond of Ireland! Then all at once,
be[cause y]ou, my dear friend, and a few more,
who are exceptions [to the g]eneral picture, have
a residence there. This it is that gives me all the
pangs I feel in seperation. I confess I carry this
spirit sometimes to the souring the pleasures I at
present possess. If I go to the opera where
Signora Colomba[6] pours out all the mazes of
melody; I sit and sigh for Lishoy fireside, and
Johnny armstrong's last good night[7] from Peggy

1 The Podareen mare was, according to the researches of Michael
  Cox (*Notes and Queries*, 8, IX, 461), the nickname of Mr Arch-
  bold's Irish Lass, who won the Royal Plate at the Curragh in
  1745 and 1748. Goldsmith was in Dublin on both occasions.
2 Percy read "one" for "[in on]e".
3 James Usher (1581–1656), Archbishop of Armagh.
4 Percy omitted "[mayb]e".
5 Percy omitted "laborious".
6 Signora Columba Mattei, a singer in the popular Italian opera.
7 Cf. *The Bee* (II, "Happiness Dependent on Constitution"): "The
  music of Matei is dissonance to what I felt when our old dairy-
  maid sang me into tears with Johnny Armstrong's Last Good

Golden. If I climb Flamstead hill where nature
never exhibited a more magnificent prospect;
I confess it fine but then I had rather be placed on
the little mount[1] before Lishoy gate, and take in,
to me, the most pleasing horizon in nature. Before
Charless came hither, as my thoughts sometimes
found refuge from severer studies among my
friends in Ireland I fancied to myself strange
revolutions at home, but I find it was the rapidity
of my own motion that gave an immaginary one
to objects really at rest. No alterations there;
some friends, he tells me, are still lean but very
rich, others very fat but still very poor nay all the
news I hear from you, is that you and Mrs. Hodson
sally out in visits among the neighbours, and
sometimes make a migration from the blue bed
to the brown[2]. I could from my heart wish that
you and She and Lishoy and Ballymahon and all
of you would fairly make a migration into Midle-
sex; tho' upon second thoughts this might be
attended with a few [in]conveniencies; therefore
as the Mountain will not come to Mahomet, why
Mahomet shall go to the Mountain, or to speak
plain english as you can not conveniently pay me

Night, or the cruelty of Barbara Allen." "Johnny Armstrong"
is also mentioned in *The Bee* (IV, "A Flemish Tradition"), and
in *The Vicar of Wakefield*, chap. IV.

1 Identified by devotees with the "neighbouring hill" of *The
Deserted Village*.
2 Cf. *The Vicar of Wakefield*, chap. I: "and all our migrations from
the blue bed to the brown."

a visit, if next Summer I can contrive to be absent six weeks from London I shall spend three of them among my friends in Ireland[1]. But first [belie]ve me my design is purely to visit, and neither to cut a [figure] nor levy contributions, neither to excite envy or [solicit charit]y[2]; in fact my circumstances are adapted to neither. [I am too] poor to be gazed at and too rich to need the assistance [of others.][3]

You see Dear Dan how long I have been talking about [myself,] but attribute my vanity to my affection; as every man is [pleasing][4] to himself, and as I consider you as second self, I immagine [you will] be consequently pleased with these instances of egotism.

Charless[5] is furnished with every thing necessary, but why [   ] stranger to assist him? I hope he will be improved in his [   ] against his return. Poor Jenny![6] But it is what I expected, My mother too has lost Pallas![7] My Dear Sir,

1 He did not carry out this plan, nor did he visit Ireland at any subsequent time before his death.
2 Percy read "solicit favour".
3 Percy read "to need assistance".
4 Percy read "fond of himself".
5 The passage "Charless. . . . Pallas!" was omitted by Percy with the comment, "Some mention of private family affairs is here omitted."
6 Jane Goldsmith, his sister, who married privately a Mr Johnson, under the impression that he was the heir of a gentleman of fortune.
7 This probably refers to the loss of a fifty-acre tract of land in

these things give me real uneasiness and I would wish to redress them. But at Present there is hardly a Kingdom in Europe in which I am not a debtor. I have already discharged my most threatening and pressing demands, for we must be just before we can be grateful. For the rest I need not say (you know I am)

Your Affectionate Kinsman

OLIVER GOLDSMITH

Temple Exchange Coffee house Near Temple Bar.
Where you may direct an answer.
December the 27th[1] 1757

VIII

To EDWARD MILLS[2]

Dᴿ Sʳ

You have quitted, I find, that plan of life which you once intended to pursue, and given

Pallas, which Mrs Goldsmith's parents had rented and endowed her with at her marriage. According to a story told by Prior (1, 9, note), she had already lost the lease of half the property, some time before the death of Jack Goldsmith, and had only succeeded in retaining the half by bribing the judge with a hundred guineas. The circumstances surrounding the loss of the remainder of the property are not known.

1 First written "25th".
2 From the original in the collection of Miss Constance Meade. It is addressed, "To Edward Mills Esqʳ near Roscommon Ireland." Edward Mills was Goldsmith's cousin, the son of Charles Goldsmith's sister. The letter was first published by Percy, in his Memoir, in 1801.

up ambition for domestic tranquillity: Were I to
consult your satisfaction alone in this change I have
the utmost reason to congratulate your choice,
but when I consider my own I cant avoid feeling
some regret, that one of my few friends has
declin'd a pursuit in which he had every reason
to expect success. The truth is, like the rest of the
world I am self-interested in my concern and do
not so much consider the happiness you have
acquir'd as the honour I have probably lost in the
change. I have often let my fancy loose when you
were the subject, and have imagined you gracing
the bench or thundering at the bar, while I have
taken no small pride to myself and whispered all
that I could come near, that that was my cousin.
Instead of this it seems you are contented to be
merely an happy man to be esteem'd only by your
acquaintance, to cultivate your paternal acres; to
take unmolested a nap under one of your own
hawthorns, or in Mrs. Mills' Bedchamber which
even a Poet must confess is rather the most comfortable place of the two.

But however your resolutions may be altered
with respect to your situation in life I persuade
my self they are unalterable with regard to your
friends in it. I can't think the world has taken
such entire possession of that heart (once so
susceptible of friendship) as not to have left a
corner there for a friend or two; Nay I flatter
myself that even I have a place among the number.

This I have a claim to from the similitude of our dispositions, or setting that aside I can demand it as my right by the most equitable law in nature, I mean that of retaliation for indeed you have more than your share in mine. I am a man of few professions, and yet this very instant I can't avoid the painful apprehension that my present professions (which speak not half my feelings) should be considered only as a pretext to cover a request, as I have a request to make. No, my dear Ned, I know you are too generous[1] to think so, and you know me too proud to stoop to mercenary insincerity. I have a request it is true to make but, as I know to whom I am a petitioner, I make it without diffidence or c[on]fusion. It is in short this: I am going to publish a book in London Entituled an Essay on the present State of Taste and Literature in Europe[2]. Every work publish'd here the Printers in Ireland republish there, without giving the Author the least consideration for his Coppy[3]. I would in this respect disappoint their avarice, and have all the additional advantages that may result from the sale of my performance there to myself. The book is now

1 Mills did not respond in any way to Goldsmith's request, as Letter xii, to Henry Goldsmith, shows.
2 The title was changed before publication to *An Enquiry into the Present State of Polite Learning in Europe.*
3 Ireland was not brought under the copyright law until the Act of Union, January 1, 1801.

printing¹ in London, and I have requested²
Doctor Radcliff³, Mr Lawder, Mr Bryanton, My
Brother Mr Henry Goldsmith, and Brother in
Law Mr Hodson to circulate my proposals among
their acquaintance; the same request I now make
to you, and have accordingly given directions to
Mr Bradley bookseller in Dame street⁴ to send you
an hundred proposals. Whatever subscriptions
pursuant to those proposals you may receive, when
collected, may be Transmitted to Mr. Bra[dley
who]⁵ will give a receipt [for the] money, and be
accountable f[or t]he books. I shall not [by a]
paltry apology excuse myself for putting you to
this troubl[e. Were] I not convincd that you
found more pleasure in doing good-n[atured]
things than uneasiness at being employd in them
I should [not have] singled you out on this
occasion. It is probable you would c[omply with]
such a request if it tended to the encouragement

---

1 He is probably anticipating the event. The book was not
published until April 2, 1759.
2 Of the three letters which survive from this group, those to
Mrs Lawder, Bryanton, and Hodson, all were written later than
this one. There is a possibility, however, that "August 7" is
a careless mistake for "August 17," since that is the date of the
letter's postmark—in which case, only the letter to Hodson is
of a later date.
3 Fellow of Trinity College, Dublin. He succeeded Theaker
Wilder as Goldsmith's tutor.
4 In Dublin.
5 The reconstructions of the bracketed portions, worn away in
the MS., are Percy's, except where otherwise noted.

of any [man of] learning whatsoever, what then
may not he expect who [has] Ties of family and
friendship to enforce his.

I am Dear Sir your Most a[ffectionate]¹

Friend and humble servant

OLIVER GOLDSMITH

London Temple Exchange Coffee house Temple Bar.
August the 7ᵗʰ 17[58.]²

IX

To ROBERT BRYANTON³

Dear Sir,

I have heard it remark'd, I believe by yourself, that they who are drunk, or out of their wits,
fancy every body else in the same condition: mine
is a friendship that neither distance nor time can

1 Percy incorrectly emended here, "your sincere".
2 The last two figures of the date, worn away in the MS., were
incorrectly supplied by Percy as "59". The mistake is probably
explained by the fact that when Percy first visited Goldsmith,
on March 3, 1759, he mistakenly recorded in his note-book that
Goldsmith was then engaged in writing his *Enquiry*. He must,
of course, have been then engaged with the proofs. See also
p. 35, note 2.
3 From Prior's *Life*, where it was first published in 1837. Prior
printed from a transcript of the original MS., given him by the
owner, Dr Handcock, of Dublin, Bryanton's son-in-law.

36

efface, which is probably the reason that, for the soul of me, I can't avoid thinking yours of the same complexion; and yet I have many reasons for being of a contrary opinion, else why in so long an absence was I never made a partner in your concerns? To hear of your successes would have given me the utmost pleasure; and a communication of your very disappointments would divide the uneasiness I too frequently feel for my own. Indeed, my dear Bob, you don't conceive how unkindly you have treated one whose circumstances afford him few prospects of pleasure, except those reflected from the happiness of his friends. However, since you have not let me hear from you, I have in some measure disappointed your neglect by frequently thinking of you. Every day do I remember the calm anecdotes of your life, from the fire-side to the easy chair; recal the various adventures that first cemented our friendship,—the school[1], the college, or the tavern; preside in fancy over your cards; am displeased at your bad play when the rubber goes against you, though not with all that agony of soul as when I once was your partner.

Is it not strange that two of such like affections should be so much separated and so differently

[1] They both attended Mr Patrick Hughes' school, at Edgeworthstown, and were contemporaries at Trinity College, Bryanton entering on November 18, 1746, a year and five months after Goldsmith.

employed as we are? You seem placed at the centre of fortune's wheel, and let it revolve never so fast, seem insensible of the motion. I seem to have been tied to the circumference, and [turned]¹ disagreeably round like an wh— in a whirligig. [I sat] down with an intention to chide, and yet methinks [I have forgot] my resentment already. The truth is, I am a [simpleton with] regard to you; I may attempt to bluster, [but like the lute of]² Anacreon, my heart is respondent only to softer affections. And yet now I think on't again, I will be angry. God's curse, Sir! who am I? Eh! what am I? Do you know whom you have offended? A man whose character may one of these days be mentioned with profound respect in a German comment or Dutch dictionary; whose name you will probably hear ushered in by a Doctissimus Doctissimorum, or heel-pieced with a long Latin termination. Think how Goldsmithius, or Gubblegurchius, or some such sound, as rough as a nutmeg-grater, will become me? Think of that!—God's curse, Sir! who am I? I must own my ill-natured cotemporaries have not hitherto paid me those honours I have had such just reason to expect. I have not yet seen my face reflected in all the lively display of red and white paints on

---

1 Unless otherwise noted, Prior's reconstructions of illegible passages are retained.
2 The reference is to the first ode of Anacreon, ΕΙΣ ΚΙΘΑΡΑΝ. Prior's reading of this lacuna was simply "but like".

any sign-posts in the suburbs. Your handkerchief weavers seem as yet unacquainted with my merits or physiognomy, and the very snuff-box makers appear to have forgot their respect. Tell them all from me, they are a set of Gothic, barbarous, ignorant scoundrels. There will come a day, no doubt it will—I beg you may live a couple of hundred years longer only to see the day—when the Scaligers[1] and Daciers[2] will vindicate my character, give learned editions of my labours, and bless the times with copious comments on the text. You shall see how they will fish up the heavy scoundrels who disregard me now, or will then offer to cavil at my productions. How will they bewail the times that suffered so much genius to lie neglected. If ever my works find their way to Tartary or China, I know the consequence. Suppose one of your Chinese Owanowitzers instructing one of your Tartarian Chianobacchi— you see I use Chinese names to show my own erudition, as I shall soon make our Chinese[3] talk

1 Julius Caesar Scaliger (1484–1558), a learned Italian critic of the Renaissance.
2 André Dacier (1651–1722) and Anne Dacier (1654–1720), his wife, famous Greek scholars who defended the cause of the Ancients in the quarrel of the Ancients and Moderns in France. Cf. *The Bee* (IV, "Miscellaneous"): "What rapture will it not give to have the Scaligers, Daciers, and Warburtons of future times...," etc.
3 This allusion shows that he was already actively planning *The Citizen of the World*, which appeared in the *Public Ledger*, under the title of *Chinese Letters*, from January, 1760, to August, 1761.

like an Englishman to show his. This may be the
subject of the lecture:—

"Oliver Goldsmith flourished in the eighteenth
and nineteenth centuries. He lived to be an
hundred and three years old, [and in that] age
may justly be styled the sun of [literature] and the
Confucius of Europe. [Many of his earlier writings,
to the regret of the] learned world, were anonymous, and have probably been lost, because
united with those of others. The first avowed piece
the world has of his is entitled an 'Essay on the
Present State of Taste and Literature in Europe,'[1]
—a work well worth its weight in diamonds. In
this he profoundly explains what learning is, and
what learning is not. In this he proves that blockheads are not men of wit, and yet that men of wit
are actually blockheads."

But as I choose neither to tire my Chinese
Philosopher, nor you, nor myself, I must dis-
continue the oration, in order to give you a good
pause for admiration; and I find myself most
violently disposed to admire too. Let me, then,
stop my fancy to take a view of my future self; and,
as the boys say, light down to see myself on horse-
back. Well, now I am down, where the d—l *is I?*
Oh, Gods! Gods! here in a garret writing for
bread, and expecting to be dunned for a milk

[1] It is worth noting that Goldsmith does not ask Bryanton's help
in soliciting subscriptions for his book, as he had declared his
intention of doing in his letter to Edward Mills.

score!¹ However, dear Bob, whether in penury
or affluence, serious or gay, I am ever wholly thine.

OLIVER GOLDSMITH

London, Temple Exchange Coffee-house,
　Temple Bar, Aug. 14, 1758.

X

To MRS. JANE LAWDER²

If you should ask, why in an interval of so many
years, you never heard from me, permit me,
Madam, to ask the same question, I have the best
excuse in recrimination. I wrote to Kilmore from

1 Forster first linked this passage with Hogarth's picture of the
Distressed Poet, and Dobson went so far as to suggest that the
picture might have been in Goldsmith's mind when he thus
described himself. That Goldsmith was familiar with Hogarth's
work at this time is certainly probable, incidental evidence
being afforded by the fact that the details of Goldsmith's
picture of Smithfield Fair, in *The Bee* (IV, "Miscellaneous"),
are identical with those of Hogarth's picture of Southwark
Fair. There is nothing, however, in the account here given
to contradict what we know of Goldsmith's circumstances at
the time, or his habits of living. He was certainly without
regular employment, was certainly writing for bread, was,
according to tradition, living in a garret in Salisbury Court,
and if we can trust a story of one of his countrymen, a Mr Pollard,
who visited him some years later (Prior, II, 192), "his constant
supper...was boiled milk."
2 From the original in the collection of Mr W. M. Elkins, of
Philadelphia. It is addressed, "To Mrs. Jane Lawder at
Kilmore near Carick-on-Shannon Ireland." Prior first published

Leyden in Holland, from Louvain in Flanders, and Rouen in France, but receivd no answer. To what could I attribute this silence but to displeasure or forgetfulness. Whether I was right in my conjecture, I do not pretend to determine, but this I must ingenuously own, that I have a thousand times in my turn endeavoured to forget them whom I could not but look upon as forgetting me. I have attempted to blot their names from my memory, and I confess it, spent whole days in efforts to tear their images from my heart; could I have succeeded you had not now been troubled with this renewal of a discontinued correspondence, but as every effort the restless make to procure sleep serves but to keep them waking, all my attempts contributed to impress what I would forget deeper on my imagination. But this is a subject I would willingly turn from, and yet for the soul of me I can't till I have said all; I was, madam, when I discontinued writing to Kilmore in such circumstances that all my endeavours to continue your regards might be attributed to wrong motives, my letters might be regarded as the petitions of a beggar and not the offerings of

it in his *Life*, in 1837, from a copy originally secured by Malone, found in the Malone-Percy correspondence, belonging at that time to Mr Mason. Malone evidently found it too late for inclusion in Percy's Memoir in 1801.

For the connection of various Goldsmith forgeries with a facsimile of this letter, published in 1858, see Appendix II, *Forged Letters*.

a friend, while all my professions insstead[1] of being considered as the result of disinterested esteem might be ascribed to venal insincerity[2]. I believe, indeed, you had too much generosity to place them in such a light, but I could not bear even the shadow of such a suspicion; the most delicate friendships are always most sensible of the slightest invasion and the strongest jealousy is ever attendant on the warmest regard. I could not, I own, I could not continue a correspondence where every acknowlegement for past favours might be considered as an indirect request for future ones[3]; and where it might be thought I gave my heart from a motive of gratitude alone when I was conscious of having bestowed it on much more disinterested principles.

It is true this conduct might have been simple[4] enough, but yourself must confess it was in character. Those who know me at all, know that I have always been actuated by different principles from the rest of Mankind, and while none regarded the interests of his friends more, no man on earth regarded his own less. I have often

1 *Sic.*
2 For the hints which this letter gives of Goldsmith's continental experiences, and of his relations with the Lawders and his uncle, see § 1 of the Introduction.
3 Cf. Letter VII, to Dan Hodson: "Too many professions of gratitude are often considered as indirect petitions for future favours."
4 He first wrote "silly" and crossed it out, perhaps because he found he had used it again below.

affected bluntness to avoid the imputation of
flattery, have frequently seem'd to overlook those
merits too obvious to escape notice, and pretended
disregard to those instances of good nature and
good sense which I could not fail tacitly to applaud;
and all this lest I should be rank'd among the
grinning tribe who say very true to all that is said,
who fill a vacant chair at a tea table whose narrow
souls never moved in a wider circle than the
circumference of a guinea, and who had rather
be reckoning the money in your pocket than the
virtue in your breast; all this, I say, I have done
and a thousand other very silly, though very disinterested things in my time, and for all which
no soul cares a farthing about me. Gods curse[1],
Madam, is it to be wondered that he should once
in his life forget you who has been all his life
forgetting him self.

However it is probable you may one of those
days see me turn'd into a perfect Hunks[2] and as
dark and intricate as a mouse-hole. I have already
given my Lanlady orders for an entire reform in
the state of my finances; I declaim against hot
suppers, drink less sugar in my tea, and cheek[3] my
grate with brick-bats. Instead of hanging my

1 Cf. the preceding letter, where this expression occurs twice.
2 A miser. Cf. *The Citizen of the World*, Letter 27, where the Man
   in Black calls himself a "saving hunks."
3 This alludes to the side-pieces, or cheeks, put into the fire-place
   to save fuel.

room with pictures I intend to adorn it with
maxims of frugality[1], these will make pretty
furniture enough and won't be a bit too expensive,
for I shall draw them all out with my own hands
and my lanlady's daughter shall frame them with
the parings of my black waistcoat[2]; Each maxim
is to be inscrib'd on a sheet of clean paper and
wrote with my best pen, of which the following
will serve as a specimen. " Look Sharp. Mind
"the mean[3] chance. Money is money now[4]. If
"you have a thousand pound, you can put your
"hands by your sides and say you are worth a
"thousand pounds every day of the year. Take
"a farthing from an hundred pound and it will
"be an hundred pound no longer."[5] Thus which
way so ever I turn my eyes they are sure to meet
one of those friendly Monitors, and as we are told

1 Cf. *The Citizen of the World*, Letter 26: "...he affects to be thought
a prodigy of parsimony and prudence; though his conversation
be replete with the most sordid and selfish maxims, his heart
is dilated with the most unbounded love."
2 Cf. the "Description of an Author's Bed Chamber," sent to
Henry in Letter xii, "The seasons fram'd with listing, found
a place." In all probability the lines were sent in the lost letter
to Henry, referred to in Letter viii, to Edward Mills, written
at approximately the same time.
3 *Sic*. This misquotation of the proverb probably resulted from
Goldsmith's Irish pronunciation of "mean" as "main."
4 Cf. *The Bee* (iii, "On the Use of Language"): "Money is
money nowadays."
5 Cf. *The Citizen of the World*, Letter 27: "If we take a farthing
from a thousand pounds it will be a thousand pounds no longer."

45

of an Actor[1] who hung his room round with looking glasses to correct the defects of his person, my appartment shall be furnished in a peculiar manner to correct the errors of my mind.

Faith! Madam, I heartily wish to be rich, if it were only for this reason, to say without a blush how much I esteem you, but alass I have many a fatigue to encounter before that happy time comes; when your poor old simple friend may again give a loose to the luxuriance of his nature, sitting by Kilmore fireside recount the various adventures of an hard fought life, laugh over the follies of the day, join his flute to your harpsicord and forget that ever he starv'd in those streets where Butler and Otway starv'd before him.

And Now I mention those great names My Uncle[2]—He is no more that soul of fire as when once I knew him. Newton and Swift grew dimn with age as well as he. But what shall I say; his mind was too active an inhabitant not to disorder the feeble mansion of its abode, for the richest jewels soonest wear their settings. Yet who but the fool would lament his condition, he now

1 Supposed to be Thomas Sheridan, the father of Richard Brinsley Sheridan. The story is retold in *The Bee* (II, "On our Theatres.") The elder Sheridan was manager of the Smock Alley Theatre in Dublin during Goldsmith's student days there.

2 His uncle probably died in this year. See § 1 of the Introduction.

46

forgets the calamities of life, perhaps indulgent heaven has given him a foretaste of that tranquillity here which he so well deserves hereafter.

But I must come to business, for business as one of my maxims tells me must be minded or lost, I am goin to publish in London A Book entituled the Present State of Taste and Literature in Europe; The Booksellers in Dublin republish every performance there without making the author any consideration I would in this respect disappoint their avarice[1] and have all the profits of my labours to myself. I must therefore request Mr. Lawder to Circulate among his friends and Acquaintance an hundred of my proposals which I have given the Bookseller.Mr Bradley in Dame Street directions to send him, if in pursuance to such circulation he should receive any subscriptions I entreat when collected they may be sent to Mr. Bradley's as aforsaid who will give a receipt and be accountable for the work or a return of the subscription. If this request, (which if complied with will in some measure be an encouragement to a man of Learning,) should be disagreable or troublesome I would not press it, for I would be the last man on earth to have my labours go a begging; but if I know Mr Lawder and sure I ought to know him, he will accept the

1 Cf. Letter vIII, to Edward Mills: "I would in this respect disappoint their avarice."

47

employment with pleasure, all I can say if he writes a book I will get him two hundred sub-scribers and those of the best witts in Europe. Whether this request is complied with or not I shall not be uneasy, but there is one Petition I must Make to him and to you which I solicit with the warmest ardour and in which I cannot bear a refusal I mean Dr Madam, That I may be always

> your Ever affectionate and obliged
> Kinsman
>
> OLIVER GOLDSMITH

You see how I blot and blunder[1]
when I am asking a favour.

Temple Exchange Coffee house near
Temple Bar. Lond. Aug^st 15th[2] 1758.

---

[1] This refers to the scratching out of the subscription. He first wrote it, "That I am always your ever affectionate obliged Kinsman, and that I may be in fact...." He then emended it to read as above.

[2] The letter was posted two days later, according to the postmark, "AU 17."

48

XI

To DANIEL HODSON[1]

[London, c. August 31, 1758][2]

Dʳ Sir

You can't expect regularity in a correspondence with one who is regular in nothing. Nay were
I forc'd to love you by rule I dare venture to say
I could never do it sincerely. Take me then with
all my faults let me write when I please, for you
see I say what I please and am only thinking aloud
when writing to you. I suppose you have heard
of my intention of going to the East Indies[3]. The
place of my destination is one of the factories on
the coast of Coromandel[4] and I go in quality of

1 From the original in the collection of Miss Constance Meade·
It is addressed, "To Daniel Hodson Esqʳ at Lishoy near Ballymahon Ireland." On the blank verso of the second page, with
the address, appears a note, written, evidently, by a family
friend, to whom the letter was sent: "Kilishee, Septemʳ 18th
1758. Mr. Piers's best Complimᵗˢ to his friends at Lisshoy. He
is obliged to them for the treat Noll's letter has afforded him.
Every line speaks the writer and is a better picture of him than
a Bindon cou'd give us of him. I long to see his book whatever
it is—And desire I may have the honour of being among the
subscribers to it." The letter was first published by Percy, in
his Memoir, in 1801.
2 The date is supplied by the postmark, "AU 31." Prior mistakenly dated it November.
3 For an account of this abortive plan, see § 3 of the Introduction.
4 On the lower south-east coast of India.

Physician and Surgeon for which the Company
has sign'd my warrant which has already cost me
ten pounds. I must also pay 50 Lb for my passage ten
pound for Sea stores, and the other incidental
expences of my equipment will amount to 60 or
70 Lb more. The Sallary is but triffling viz 100 Lb
per ann. but the other advantages if a person be
prudent are considerable. The practice of the
place if I am rightly informed generally amounts
to not less than one thousand pounds per ann. for
which the appointed Physician has an exclusive
privelege, this with the advantages resulting from
trade with the high interest which money bears
viz 20 per cent. are the inducements which
persuade me to undergo the fatigues of sea the
dangers of war and the still greater dangers of the
climate, which induce me to leave a place where
I am every day gaining friends[1] and esteem and
where I might enjoy all the conveniencies of life.
I am certainly wrong not to be contented with
what I already possess triffling as it is, for should
I ask myself one serious question what is it I want?
What can I answer? My desires are as capricious
as the big bellied woman's who longd for a piece
of her husband's nose. I have no certainty it is
true; but why can't I do as some men of more
merit who have liv'd upon more precarious terms?

1 Who his friends were at this time is uncertain. He knew
Grainger, certainly, and may have known Smollett, Murphy,
Burke, and Johnson. He met Percy the following March.

Scaron us'd jestingly to call himself the Lord
Marquis of Quenault[1] which was the name of the
bookseller who employ'd him, and why may not
I assert my privelege and quality on the same
pretensions? Yet upon deliberation, whatever
airs I may give myself on this side of the water,
my dignity I fancy would be evaporated before
I reach'd the other. I know you have in Ireland
a very indifferent Idea of a man who writes for
bread. tho Swift and Steel did so in the earlier
part of their lives. You Imagine, I suppose, that
every author by profession lives in a garret, wears
shabby cloaths, and converses with the meanest
company; but I assure you such a character is
entirely chimerical. Nor do I believe there is one
single writer, who has abilities to translate a french
Novel[2], that does not keep better company wear
finer cloaths and live more genteely than many
who pride themselves for nothing else in Ireland.
I confess it again my Dear Dan that nothing but
the wildest ambition could prevail on me to
leave the enjoyment of that refined conversation
which I sometimes am admitted to partake in for

1 Should be "Quinet" (Sells, *Sources Françaises de Goldsmith*, p. 38).
2 Prior and others have thought that this alluded to *Memoirs of
My Lady B*, a lost work, translated for Griffiths. The supposition
cannot be correct, since the translation appears in the list of
new books in the *Gentleman's Magazine* for January, 1761, and the
original itself, *Memoires de Milady B*, by Mlle Charlotte-Marie-
Anne Charbonnier de la Guesnerie, was not published until
1760.

uncertain fortune and paltry shew. You can't conceive how I am sometimes divided, to leave all that is dear gives me pain, but when I consider that it is possible I may acquire a genteel independance for life, when I think of that dignity which Philosophy claims to raise it above contempt and ridicule, when I think thus, I eagerly long to embrace every opportunity of separating myself from the vulgar, as much in my circumstances as I am in my sentiments already.

I am going to publish a book for an account of which I refer you to a le[tter][1] which I wrote to my Brother Goldsmith. Circulate for me among your acquaintance an hundred proposals which I have given orders may be sent to you. and if in pursuance of such circulation you should receive any subscriptions let them when collected be transmitted to Mr Bradley who will give a receipt for the same[2]. I am very much pleasd with the accounts you send me of your little son[3]; if I do

1 The bracketed portions, worn away in the MS., follow Percy's conjectural reconstructions, unless otherwise noted.
2 The remainder of the letter—with the exception of "I know not how my desire...conscious of them"—was omitted by Percy, with the statement, "Omitting here what relates to private family affairs he then adds:". The omitted passage, with the exception of the scored-out lines, which are here printed for the first time, was printed by Clarke (*Trans. Bib. Soc.* xv, 26).
3 William Hodson, whom Goldsmith afterwards befriended greatly. See Letters xxv, xxvi, xxxi, and xxxix.

not mistake that was his hand which subscrib'd itself Gilbeen Hardly. There is nothing could please me more than a letter filld with all the news of the country, but I fear you will think that too troublesome. You see I never cease writing 'till a whole sheet of paper is wrote out, I beg you will immitate me in this particular and give your letters good measure. You can tell me, what visits you receive or pay, who has been married or debauch'd, since my absence what fine girls you have starting up and beating of the vetterans of my acquaintance from future conquest. I suppose before I return I shall find all the blooming virgins I once left in Westmeath shrivelled into a parcel of hags with seven children a piece tearing down their petticoats. Most of the Bucks and Bloods whom I left hunting and drinking and swearing and getting bastards I find are dead. Poor devils they kick'd the world before them. I wonder what the devil they kick now?

Dear Sister I wrote to Kilmore[1] I wish you would let me know how that family stands affected with regard to me. My Brother Charles promis'd to tell me all about it but his letter gave me no satisfaction in those particulars. I beg you and Dan would put your hands to the oar and fill me a sheet with somewhat or other, if you can't

---

1 He refers to the letter to Jane Lawder, written on August 15, evidently at his sister's behest.

get quite thro your selves lend Billy or Nancy the
pen and let the dear little things give me their
nonsense. Talk all about yourselves and nothing
about me. You see I do so. I know not how my
desire of seeing Ireland which has so long slept
has again revivd with so much ardour. So weak
is my temper and so unsteady that I am frequently
tempted, particularly [when low] spirited, to
return home and leave my fortune tho' just [now
it is be]ᵗginning to look kinder. But It shall not
be. In five or si[x years] I hope to indulge these
transports, I find I want constitution, [and a]
strong steady disposition which alone makes men
great, I [will how]ever correct my faults since I am
conscious of them. I [hope]¹ brother Charles is
settled to business. I see no probability of h[is
succeeding in]¹ any other method of proceeding².
Maurice³ I find wan[ts   ]¹ I am sorry for it.
But what can be done since he neith[er can write
nor]¹ spell with tolerable propriety. As for going
with m[e that is im]¹possible his verry passage
expences and all would cost one hundred pounds.
If he would accustom himself to write and spell
I will end[ea]¹vour to procure him some employ-

1 Supplied by the editor.
2 The passage "Maurice I find…sending for him to live with me"
  is carefully scratched out in the MS. in ink of a lighter shade.
  Maurice himself probably did it before sending the letter to
  Percy in 1776. Cf. the scored out passage in the following
  letter.
3 His brother, the fifth child.

ment in London. In about two months with diligence and care he might gain a tolerable proficiency in those qualifications and if when so qualified he would send me a specimen of his performance which I might show to his employer I hope I will get him some thing or other unless he might think it beneath him to stoop to little things in the beginning. What money may be necessary to carry him to London shall be supply'd him by a correspondent at Chester[1], and his prudence and submissive behaviour in this station may be a means of his meeting something better in time to come, Or if I succeed according to my expectation where I am going, of my sending for him to live with me. Pray let me hear from my Mother since she will not gratify me herself and tell me if in anything I can be immediately servicable to her. Tell me how My Brother Gold-smith and his Bishop agree. Pray do this for me for heaven knows I would do anything to serve you.

1 This may be the Doctor Keay of Chester, referred to in Letter xv, to Mrs Johnson. Who he was, or how he happened to be under a money obligation to Goldsmith, is not known.

XII

To the Reverend HENRY GOLDSMITH[1]

[London, c. January 13, 1759][2]

Dear Sir,

Your Punctuality in answering a man whose trade is writing, is more than I had reason to expect; and yet you see me generally fill a whole sheet, which is all the recompence I can make for being so frequently troublesome. The behaviour of Mr Mills and Mr Lawder is a little extraordinary, however their answering neither you nor me is a sufficient indication of their disliking the employment which I assign'd them. As their conduct is different from what I had expected so I have made an alteration in mine. I shall the beginning of next month send over two hundred and fifty books which is all that I fancy can be well sold among you. And I would have you make some distinction in the persons who have subscrib'd. The money which will ammount to sixty pounds may be left with Mr. Bradley as soon as possible I am not certain but I shall quickly have

---

1 From the original in the collection of Miss Constance Meade. It is addressed, "To The Revd Henry Goldsmith, at Lowfield, near Ballymore in Westmeath, Ireland." It was first published by Percy, in his Memoir, in 1801.

2 The date is supplied by the postmark, "13 IA." The letter has been supposed by former editors to date from about the first of February.

occasion for it. I have met with no disappointment with respect to my East India Voyage[1] nor
are my resolutions altered, tho' at the same time
I must confess it gives me some pain to think I am
almost beginning the world at the age of thrty[2]
one[3]. Tho' I never had a day's sickness since I saw
you yet I am not that strong active man you once
knew me. You scarce can conceive how much
eight years of disappointment anguish and study
have worn me down. If I remember right you
are seven or eight years older than me, and yet
I dare venture to say that if a stranger saw us
both he would pay me the honours of seniority.
Immagine to yourself a pale melancholly visage
with two great wrinkles between the eye brows,
with an eye disgustingly severe and a big wig,
and you may have a perfect picture of my present
appearance. On the other hand I conceive you

1 See § 3 of the Introduction.   2 *Sic.*
3 Goldsmith's allusion to his age here was considered by Percy
  as corroboration of Maurice Goldsmith's statement that his
  brother was born in 1728 (see the editor's *Percy's Memoir of Goldsmith*, p. 13, note 4). If Goldsmith's remark here is to be taken
  as proof, we must assume, not 1728 as the birth year, but 1727,
  since his thirty-first birthday would have been in November,
  1758. This runs counter to all the other evidence, which is too
  complicated and extensive to be presented here, but which
  may be said, in brief, to point to 1730 as the actual date. The
  editor believes that the contrary evidence is weighty enough to
  challenge even as authoritative a statement as this one, from
  Goldsmith's own pen. The argument will be presented *in
  extenso* elsewhere.

as grown fat sleek and healthy, passing many an happy day among your own children or those who knew you a child. Since I knew what it was to be a man this is a pleasure I have not known. I have passd my days among a number of cool designing beings and have contracted all their suspicious manner, in my own behaviour. I should actually be as unfit for the society of my friends at home as I detest that which I am obliged to partake of here. I can now neither partake of the pleasure of a revel nor contribute to raise its jollity, I can neither laugh nor drink, have contracted an hesitating disagreeable manner of speaking, and a visage that looks illnature itself, in short I have thought myself into settled melancholly and an utter disgust of all that life brings with it. Whence this romantic turn that all our family are possessed with, whence this love for every place and every country but that in which we reside? For every occupation but our own, this desire of fortune and yet this eagerness to dissipate! I perceive my dear Sir, that I am at intervals for indulging this splenetic manner and following my own taste regardless of yours. The reasons you have given me for breeding up your son[1] a scholar are

1 Henry Goldsmith, Jr., who could not have been more than three years old at this time. He went to America as Lieutenant in the British army in 1775, was wounded, and later married the Rhode Island lady who nursed him. He settled permanently in Nova Scotia and there brought up his family (*Notes and Queries*, 12, IV, 177).

judicious and convincing. I should however be
glad to know for what particular profession he is
design'd? If he be assiduous, and divested of
strong passions[1], (for passions in youth always
lead to pleasure) he may do very well in your
college, for it must be ownd that the industrious
poor have good encouragement there, perhaps
better than in any other in Europe. But if he
has ambition, strong passions, and an exquisite
sensibility of contempt[2], do not send him there,
unless you have no other trade for him except
your own. It is impossible to conceive how much
may be done by a proper education at home.
A boy, for instance, who understands perfectly
well Latin, French, Arithmetic and the principles
of the civil law[3], and can write a fine hand[4], has

1 Cf. *The Present State of Polite Learning*, chap. IX: "A lad whose
  passions are not strong enough...may probably obtain every
  advantage and honour his college can bestow."
2 Cf. *ibid.* chap. IX: "His simplicity exposes him to all the insidious approaches of cunning; his sensibility, to the slightest
  invasions of contempt. Though possessed of fortitude to stand
  unmoved the expected bursts of an earthquake, yet of feelings
  so exquisitely poignant as to agonize under the slightest disappointment."
3 Isaac Reed and Seward are authorities for the statement
  (Prior, II, 156) that Goldsmith was an unsuccessful candidate in
  1767 for the Graham lectureship in Civil Law. When he
  studied law is not known.
4 The clause, "and can write a fine hand," is added with a caret
  between the lines. The thought of Maurice's predicament must
  have prompted the addition.

an education that may qualify him for any undertaking. And these parts of learning should be
carefully inculcated let him be designed for whatsoever calling he will. Above all things· let him
never touch a romance[1], or novel, those paint
beauty in colours more charming than nature, and
describe happiness that man never tastes. How
delusive, how destructive therefore are those
pictures of consummate bliss, they teach the
youthful mind to sigh after beauty and happiness
which never existed, to despise the little good which
fortune has mixed in our cup, by expecting more
than she ever gave. And in general take the word
of a man who has seen the world, and studied
human nature more by experience than precept,
take my word for it I say that books teach us very
little of the world[2]. The greatest merit, and the
most consummate virtue that ever grac'd humanity
in a state of poverty would only serve to make the
possessor ridiculous[3], they may distress but can-

1 Cf. *The Citizen of the World*, Letter 83: ' I say with them that
every book can serve to make us more expert, except romances,
and these are no better than instruments of debauchery," etc.
The whole passage on the dangers of romances for the young is
not Goldsmith's own, but a quotation, as his note indicates,
from Du Halde's *Description of the Empire of China* (London,
Edward Cave, 1738–41, II, 58).

2 Cf. *The Citizen of the World*, Letter 67, for similar opinions on
a "book-taught philosopher."

3 Cf. *The Present State of Polite Learning*, chap. IX: "For all the wit
that ever adorned the human mind will at present no more
shield the author's poverty from ridicule."

not relieve him. Avarice[1] in the lower orders of mankind is true ambition, avarice is the only ladder the poor can use to preferment. Preach, then my dear Sir, to your son, not the excellence of human nature, nor the disrespect of riches, but endeavour to teach him thrift and œconomy. Let his poor wandering uncles example be placd in his eyes. I had learn'd from books to love virtue, before I was taught from experience the necessity of being selfish. I had contracted the habits and notions of a Philosopher, while I was exposing myself to the insidious approaches of cunning[2]; and often, by being even from my narrow finances charitable to excess, I forgot the rules of justice, and placd myself in the very situation of the wretch who thank'd my bounty[3]. When I am in the remotest part of the world tell him this and perhaps he may improve by my example. But I find myself again falling into my gloomy habits of thinking[4]. Prithee why does not

1 Cf. *The Bee* (III, "On Justice and Generosity," v, "Upon Political Frugality" and VI, "On Education") for parallels to this advice.

2 See note 2, p. 59.

3 Cf. *The Bee* (III, "On Justice and Generosity"): "Thus he is induced, by misplaced generosity to put himself into the indigent circumstances of the person he relieves." If the story is true that Goldsmith had at this time pawned Griffiths' clothes to secure his landlady's husband from a debtors' prison, this must be a direct allusion to that circumstance.

4 The passage "Prithee why does not Maurice...every day open." is carefully scored out in the original MS., and can be read only

Maurice send *me* his [writing?] I could [put] him in a way of getting his bread. If he should want about five pounds to carry him up to London Pray let him have it when you receive it for me and if the Poor lad wants cloaths I believe mine will fit him so let not that retard his diligence. I don't want to have him here in order to make him unhappy. I have taken a chambers in the temple[1] and he shall lodge with me until something is provided, for places of the sort for which I intend him, every day open. My Mother I am informed is almost blind, even tho' I had the utmost inclination to return home I could not, to behold her in distress without a capacity of relieving her from it, would be too much to add to my present splenetic habit. Your last letter was much too short, it should have answered some queries I had made in my former. Just sit down as I do, and write forward 'till you have filld all your paper, it requires no thought, at least if I may judge from the ease with which my own sentiments rise when they are addressd to you. For believe me my head has no share in all I write my heart

with difficulty. It is here printed for the first time. Maurice himself probably made the excision before sending the letter to Percy in 1776.

1 That Goldsmith had chambers in the Temple at this time has not previously been known. His residence there must have been temporary, for Percy entered Goldsmith's address in his diary for February 21, 1759, as "Mrs. Martin's in Green Arbour Court, Little Old Bayley."

dictates the whole. Pray give my love to Bob Bryanton and entreat him from me not to drink. My Dear Sir give me some account about poor Jenny. Yet her husband loves her, if so she cannot be unhappy.

I know not whether I should tell you, yet why should I conceal those triffles, or indeed any thing from you, there is a book[1] of mine will be publish'd in a few days. The life of a very extraordinary man. No less than the great Mr. Voltaire. You know already by the title that it is no more than a catch-penny. However I spent but four weeks on the whole performance for which I receiv'd twenty pound. When publish'd I shall take some method of conveying it to you, unless you may think it dear of the postage which may ammount to four or five shillings, however I fear you will not find an equivalence of amusement. Your last letter, I repeat it, was too short, you should have given me your opinion of the design of the heroicomical poem which I sent you. You remember I intended to introduce the hero of the Poem as lying in

1 This work was advertised as "speedily to be published" on February 7, in the *Public Advertiser* (Prior, I, 304) but no copies of it are known to exist. A life of Voltaire, which Prior believes to be identical with this, was published by Goldsmith in the *Lady's Magazine* for 1761. Prior (I, 288) supposed that by writing this "catchpenny," Goldsmith paid the debt to Griffiths which forms the subject of the following letter; but the earlier date established for this letter by the postmark makes this theory manifestly untenable.

a paltry alehouse you may take the following
specimen of the manner; which I flatter myself is
quite original. The room [in] which he lies may
be descri[bed] somewhat this way.

[A]¹ Window patch'd with paper lent a ray,
That feebly shew'd the state in which he lay.
The sanded floor, that grits beneath the tread
The humid wall with paltry pictures spread.
The game of goose² was there expos'd to view,
And the twelve rules³ the Royal Martyr drew.
The seasons⁴ fram'd with listing, found a place,
And Prussia's Monarch⁵ shew'd his lamp black face.

1 Used later, with changes, in *The Citizen of the World*, Letter 30.
  Some details of the description also recur in *The Deserted Village*,
  ll. 227–36.
2 A game somewhat like modern parchesi, played with a teetotum
  or dice. *Larousse Illustré*, under "oie," gives a picture of the
  game board, and directions for playing, and adds that in the
  eighteenth century it was played "non seulement par les enfants
  comme de nos jours, mais encore par les grandes personnes et
  dans la meilleure société."
3 King Charles' Twelve Golden Rules. "1. Urge no healths.
  2. Profane no divine ordinance. 3. Touch no state matters.
  4. Reveal no secrets. 5. Pick no quarrels. 6. Make no com-
  parisons. 7. Maintain no ill opinions. 8. Keep no bad company.
  9. Encourage no vice. 10. Make no long meals. 11. Repeat no
  grievances. 12. Lay no wagers."
4 At least four sets of "Seasons" in mezzotint were published
  about the year 1759, any one of which Goldsmith may have had
  in mind: James McArdell's, after Bowles; Richard Houston's,
  after Mercier; Remigius Parr's, after Lancret; and Richard
  Purcell's ("Charles Corbutt"), after Pyle. The editor is indebted for this information to Miss E. W. Manwaring.
5 Frederick the Great, whose popularity in England was at its

The morn was cold he views with keen desire,
A rusty grate unconscious of a fire.
An unpaid reck'ning on the freeze was scor'd,
And five crack'd teacups dress'd the chimney
   [board.]
   And Now immagine after his soliloquy the land-
lord to make his appearance in order to Dun him
for the reckoning,
Not with that face so servile and so gay
That welcomes every stranger that can pay,
With sulky eye he smoak'd the patient man
Then pull'd his breeches tight, and thus began, &c.
All this is taken you see from Nature. It is a Good
remark of Montaign's that the wisest men often
have friends with whom they do not care how
much they play the fool. Take my present follies
as instances of regard. Poetry is much an easier
and more agreeable species of composition than
prose, and could a man live by it[1], it were no

height in 1758–9. In the *Citizen of the World* version, published
in the *Public Ledger* in 1760, "brave Prince William" (the Duke
of Cumberland) replaces him.
[1] Bishop White of Pennsylvania records in his autobiography
a conversation with Goldsmith on this subject in 1770, in which
a very different opinion is expressed. On being asked why he
did not set forth in a pamphlet his views on the decay of the
peasantry expressed in *The Deserted Village*, Goldsmith replied,
"It is not worth my while. A good poem will bring me a
hundred guineas, but the pamphlet would bring me nothing"
(J. H. Ward, *Life and Times of Bishop White*, p. 24). This lends
weight to Cooke's statement that the original payment for *The
Deserted Village* was a hundred guineas.

unpleasant employment to be a Poet. I am re-
solvd to leave no space tho' I should fill it up only
by telling you what you very well know already, I
mean that I am your most affectionate friend and
Brother.

OLIVER GOLDSMITH

XIII

To RALPH GRIFFITHS[1]

Sir,   [London, January, 1759][2]

I know of no misery but a gaol to which my own
imprudencies and your letter seem to point. I have
seen it inevitable this three or four weeks, and by
heavens, request it as a favour, as a favour that
may prevent somewhat more fatal. I have been

1 From the original in the Victoria and Albert Museum, South
  Kensington. It was first published by Prior, in his *Life*, in 1837.
  The reader is referred to Prior (I, 283–8) for the circumstances
  surrounding the writing of this letter. Griffiths was the pro-
  prietor of the *Monthly Review*.
2 The date is supplied from Griffiths' endorsement: "Rec'd in
  Jany. 1759." It seems clear that it was written after the preceding letter to Henry: the "three or four weeks" of the second
  sentence must allude to the lapse of time since his rejection
  at Surgeon's Hall, on December 21, which would make the
  earliest possible date for this letter January 11; and to assume
  that Goldsmith wrote his long, discursive letter to his brother
  on January 13, in the very shadow of a debtor's jail, without
  betraying his acute anxiety, seems highly improbable, although
  the tenor of the letter does, indeed, show that he recognized his
  financial difficulties. It seems plausible, therefore, to date the
  letter shortly after January 13.

66

some years struggling with a wretched being, with all that contempt which indigence brings with it, with all those strong passions which make contempt insupportable. What then has a gaol that is formidable, I shall at least have the society of wretches, and such is to me true society. I tell you again and again I am now neither able nor willing to pay you a farthing, but I will be punctual to any appointment you or the taylor shall make; thus far at least I do not act the sharper [1], since unable to pay my debts one way I would willingly give some security another. No Sir, had I been a sharper, had I been possessed of less good nature and native generosity I might surely now have been in better circumstances. I am guilty I own of meanessess [2] which poverty unavoidably brings with it [3], my reflections are filld with repentance for my imprudence but not with any remorse for being a villain, that may be a character you unjustly charge me with. Your books I can assure you are neither pawn'd nor

1 Kenrick, in his malevolent review of Goldsmith's *Present State of Polite Learning*, printed in the *Monthly Review* for November, 1759, repeats the two charges of his having played the sharper and acted with ingratitude. Kenrick was obviously Griffiths' mouthpiece in the matter.

2 *Sic.*

3 Cf. *The Citizen of the World*, Letter 83: "and avoids all those meannesses which indigence sometimes unavoidably produces." This in turn was a variation on a passage in Du Halde (II, 46): "and being exempted from these meannesses, he maintains his rank, and makes himself respected."

sold, but in the custody of a friend from whom my necessities oblig'd me to borrow some money, whatever becomes of my person, you shall have them in a month. It is very possible both the reports you have heard and your own suggestions may have brought you false information with respect to my character, it is very possible that the man whom you now regard with detestation may inwardly burn with grateful resentment, it is very possible that upon a second perusal of the letter I sent you, you may see the workings of a mind strongly agitated with gratitude[1] and jealousy, if such circumstances should appear at least spare invective 'till my book with Mr. Dodsley shall be publish'd, and then perhaps you may see the bright side of a mind when my professions shall not appear the dictates of necessity but of choice. You seem to think Doctor Milner[2] knew me not. Perhaps so; but he was a man I shall ever honour; but I have friendship only with the dead! I ask pardon for taking up so much time. Nor shall I add to it by any other professions than that I am Sir your Humble serv.^t

OLIVER GOLDSMITH

P.S. I shall expect impatiently the result of your resolutions[3].

1 See n. 1, p. 67.
2 The head of the Peckham School, at whose table Goldsmith first met Griffiths. He died some time in 1758.
3 Goldsmith's biographers have assumed that after Kenrick's attack in November Goldsmith never afterwards renewed his

XIV

To MRS. JOHNSON[1]

[London, ? 1760][2]

Mr. Goldsmith's best respects to Mrs. Johnson will pay a Guinea or whatever she thinks proper either of his own or her appointing only letting him know to whom or for what: He will wait on Mrs. Johnson if she thinks proper this evening at six, or if, as she intended she will call upon him he will be very proud of that honour. A line or two by the bearer will not be amiss.

connection with Griffiths. His translation of *Memoirs of My Lady B*, in 1760 (see note 2, p. 51), disproves this.

1 From a transcript of the original in the collection of Mr R. B. Adam, of Buffalo. It has previously been printed only in the catalogue of Mr Adam's library. It is endorsed on the verso, in a hand not Goldsmith's, "To Mrs. Johnson." The lady's identity is unknown, as is also the nature of the transaction involving a guinea, to which this and the following note refer.
2 The reasons for assigning this conjectural date will be found in note 2 to the following letter.

XV

To MRS. JOHNSON[1]

[London, ?1760][2]

Dear Madam

I sent word to Doctor Keay of Chester to pay
Faulkener[3] a guinea I receiv'd no answer from
him but I believe it is paid. I shall write again
tonight. If you chuse I will return you the guinea.

I am your

humble servant

OLIVER GOLDSMITH

1 From the original in the possession of Mr A. S. W. Rosenbach
of New York, never before published. The recipient is known
only through the endorsement, pencilled on the verso in a
modern hand, "To Mrs. Johnson," and through the note's
obvious reference to the same transaction mentioned in the
preceding note. Besides the endorsement on the verso, there
appears a memorandum, in an eighteenth-century hand,
scratched over, and partially illegible: "There is a 3 or 400 pds
worth of things brought in to the House which...no person."

2 The date of the two notes is conjectural. The use of "Mr. Goldsmith" in Letter xiv indicates a period before 1763, since after
that date his almost constant practice was to refer to himself as
"Dr. Goldsmith." The probability that the Dr Keay referred
to here is identical with the Chester correspondent mentioned
in Letter xi suggests a date near 1758. See also note 3.

3 Possibly George Faulkener, the Dublin publisher, who came to
London on a visit in 1760.

XVI

To JOHN NEWBERY[1]

[London, early summer, 1762][2]

Dr Sir,

As I have been out of order for some time past and am still not quite recovered the fifth volume of Plutarch's lives[3] remains unfinish'd, I fear I shall not be able to do it, unless there be an actual necessity and that none else can be found, If therefore you would send it to Mr Collier[4] I should esteem it a kindness, and will pay for

1 From the original in the possession of Mr. W. M. Elkins, of Philadelphia. It forms a part of the Newbery collection of Goldsmith papers, and was first published by Prior, in his *Life*, in 1837. It is addressed, "To Mr. Newbery, St. Paul's Church Yard."

2 The date is conjectural. Gibbs dated this and the following note "March, 1762," on the evidence of Goldsmith's receipt to Newbery, for eleven and one-half guineas for "an abridgement of Plutarch's Lives," dated March 5, 1762. That receipt was clearly for the first two volumes, while this note refers to a subsequent payment of twelve guineas, presumably for the third and fourth.

3 This compilation, which ran only to seven volumes, was originally intended to comprise all ancient and modern biography. Prior conjectured that the success of Dilly's *British Plutarch*, appearing at this time, was the reason for curtailing the plan.

4 Joseph Collyer, a translator and literary compiler, was the author of *A New System of Geography*, translator of Bodmer's *Noah*, etc.

whatever it may come to. N.B. I received twelve guineas for the two Volumes.

I am Sir your obliged humble serv^t

OLIVER GOLDSMITH

Pray let me have an answer.

XVII

To JOHN NEWBERY[1]

[London, early summer, 1762][2]

Sir

One Volume is done namely the fourth; When I said I should be glad Mr Collier would do the fifth for me, I only demanded it as a favour, but if he cannot conveniently do it tho I have kept my chamber these three weeks and am not yet quite recovered yet I will do it. I send it[3] per bearer, and if the affair puts you to the least inconvenience return it, and it shall be done immediately. I am, &c.

O. G.

The Printer has the Copy of the rest.

1 From the original in the possession of Mr. W. M. Elkins, of Philadelphia. The history of the text is identical with that of the preceding letter, which it follows shortly in point of time It is addressed " To Mr. Newbery."
2 See note 2 of the preceding letter.
3 The unfinished fifth volume.

XVIII

To JAMES DODSLEY[1]

Gray's Inn[2]

Sir

I shall take it as a favour if you can let me have ten guineas per bearer, for which I promise to account. I am sir your humble servant,

OLIVER GOLDSMITH

March 10, 1764.

PS I shall call to see you on Wednesday next with copy[3] &c.

1 From the original in the collection of Mr W. M. Elkins, of Philadelphia. It was first published by Forster, in his *Life of Goldsmith*. It is addressed, "To Mr. Dodesley, Pall Mall."
2 This heading is the only evidence for Goldsmith's place of residence between his leaving Mrs Fleming's in Islington, on December 25, 1763, and returning there on March 29, 1764 (Forster, 1, 345).
3 Probably this copy was of a history of England, which Goldsmith wrote for Dodsley some time in 1764, and which Dodsley included in an anonymous volume, published in 1765, entitled *The Geography and History of England done in the manner of Gordon's and Salmon's Geographical and Historical Grammars*. Goldsmith's history follows the geographical portion, and is clearly distinguishable as his by its style. The authorship of the book, which has only recently come to light, was first revealed by Goldsmith's receipt to Dodsley, now the property of Mr. W. G. Tegg, of Rothley, near Leicester, England: "Received from Mr. James Dodsley thirty guineas for writing and compiling an history of England, August 8th, 1764.—Oliver Goldsmith.'

XIX

To GEORGE COLMAN[1]

Temple, Garden Court, July 19th [1767][2]
Dear Sir,

I am very much obliged to you, both for your kind partiality in my favour, and your tenderness in shortening the interval of my expectation. That the play[3] is liable to many objections I well know, but I am happy that it is in hands the most capable in the world of removing them. If then Dear Sir, you will complete your favours by putting the

1 From the original in the Victoria and Albert Museum, South Kensington. It is addressed, "To George Colman Esqr Richmond." It was found among the papers of Mr Morris, Colman's successor as manager of the Haymarket, and was lent by Morris' executors to Forster, who first published it in his *Life of Goldsmith*, in 1848.

2 This heading is the sole evidence for Goldsmith's place of residence in town between his leaving the chambers in King's Bench Walk and his permanent settlement in No. 2, Brick Court, at the end of this year.

3 *The Good-Natured Man.* The circumstances surrounding its acceptance by Colman are well known. He had severed his connection with Garrick and Drury Lane the previous spring, and, in partnership with Rutherford and Harris, had bought the patents of Covent Garden from the widow of Rich, and had assumed the managership. His first act as manager, as was revealed in a law-suit brought against him by his partners in 1769, was to over-step the bounds of his authority by accepting Goldsmith's play without their concurrence (Wyndham, *Annals of Covent Garden Theatre,* I, 169).

piece into such a state as it may be acted, or of directing me how to do it I shall ever retain a sense of your goodness to me. And indeed tho' most probably this be the last I shall ever write yet I can't help feeling a secret satisfaction that poets for the future are likely to have a protector who declines taking advantage of their dependent situation[1], and scorns that importance which may be acquir'd by triffling with their anxieties[2].

I am Dear Sir with the greatest esteem your most obedient humble servant.

OLIVER GOLDSMITH

1 The stringency of his finances at this time is evidenced by the fact that on July 7 he had borrowed £10 of Newbery on a promissory note, with a note of £48, dating from October 11, 1763, still unpaid.
2 A palpable allusion to Garrick.

XX

To DAVID GARRICK[1]

London July 20th 1767

Sir

A few days ago Mr. Beard[2] renewd his claim to the piece which I had written for his stage, and had as a friend submitted to your perusal. As

---

1 From the original in the New York Public Library. It is addressed, "To David Garrick Esqr. at Litchfield," on the verso of the second sheet, and on the recto of that sheet appears a draft of Garrick's reply, in his own hand:

My answer   *Lichfield July* 25 1767.

Sr. I was at Birmingham when yr. letter came to this place, or I shd. have thank'd you for it immediately—I was indeed much hurt that yr warmth at our last meeting mistook my sincere & friendly attention to yr. Play for ye remains of a former misunderstanding wch. I had as much forgot as if it never had existed—What I said to you at my own house, I now repeat, that I felt more pain in giving my Sentiments than you possibly could in receiving them. It has been ye business & ambition of my Life to live upon ye best terms wth Men of Genius, & as I know that Dr. Goldsmith will have no reason to change his present friendly disposition towards me, so I shall be glad of any future opportunity to convince him how much

I am his obedt. Serv. & well wisher

D. Garrick.

The letter, and Garrick's answer, were first published by Prior, in his *Life*, in 1837.

2 John Beard, the singer, Rich's son-in-law, and acting manager of Covent Garden since Rich's death. He had resigned his managership to Colman on May 14 (Foot, *Life of Arthur Murphy*, p. 347), and Goldsmith's reason for using his name here is not clear, unless, as Forster suggests, to spare Garrick's feelings the reminder of Colman's defection from Drury Lane.

76

I found you had very great difficulties about that piece I complied with his desire, thinking it wrong to take up the attention of my friends[1] with such petty concerns as mine or to load your good nature by a compliance rather with their requests than my merits: I am extremely sorry that you should think me warm at our last meeting, your judgement certainly ought to be free especially in a matter which must in some measure concern your own credit and interest[2]. I assure you Sir I have no disposition to differ with you on this or any other account, but am with an high opinion of your abilities and with a very real esteem Sir

Your most obedient humble serv[t]

OLIVER GOLDSMITH

1 Probably Reynolds and Johnson. Prior refers to a letter "still in existence" from Reynolds to Garrick, bringing him and Goldsmith together, and states further, on unnamed authority, that Johnson and Reynolds were told by Garrick that the play would not succeed on presentation.

2 This hint corroborates the account which Davies gives of the real cause of disagreement: "Mr. Garrick...expected the writer should esteem the patronage of his play as a favour: Goldsmith rejected all ideas of kindness in a bargain that was intended to be of mutual advantage to both parties; and in this he was certainly justifiable" (*Life of Garrick*, II, 146).

77

XXI

To MRS ANNE PERCY[1]

[Early January, 1768][2]

Doctor Goldsmith's best respects to Mrs. Percy he requests the favour of two tickets for two young Ladies for the Masquerade which is to be on Friday night. If she can procure them for him it will be a singular obligation, and make two young Ladies extremely happy. I have not seen Mr. Percy for some time, but hope this winter we shall frequently have the happiness of being together[3].

Teusday[4]. Temple. Brick Court.

1 From the original in the collection of Miss Constance Meade. It is addressed, "To Mrs. Percy at the Queen's Palace." It was first published by Miss Gaussen in *Percy, Prelate and Poet*, in 1908.
2 The date is conjectural. It must fall within the year of Mrs Percy's service in the royal household as nurse to the infant Prince Edward, Duke of Kent, which began on November 2, 1767. It must also fall after Goldsmith's removal to his new quarters in Brick Court, the exact date of which is not known, but which evidently took place before the first of the year, since Filby rendered his 1767 bill to "Mr. Oliver Goldsmith, Dr., Brick Court, Temple, up two pairs of stairs." And it apparently preceded Goldsmith's first meeting with Percy that winter, which, according to Percy's diary (B.M. Add. MS. 32,336), took place at least as early as January 4, at Reynolds' house.
3 He may be anticipating here Percy's election to the Club, which took place on February 15 of this year.
4 *Sic.*

XXII

To the Reverend THOMAS PERCY[1]

Dear Percy   [London, early in 1768][2]

I have been thinking of your Northamptonshire offer. I beg you'l send me an answer to the
following Queries.

1. In the first place are there any prying troublesome neighbours?
2. Can I have a chamber to myself where I can
buy coals, &c?
3. Will I not cumber the house and take up the
room of others?[3]
4. How long can you spare the appartment?
5. Is there a stage? The price. And can my
books[4] be carried down.
6. Can I have milk, meat, &c tea, in the place?
And lastly will it be any way inconvenient to

1 From the original in the collection of Miss Constance Meade.
It is addressed, "To the Rev^d Mr. Percy Northumberland-house."
It was first published by Miss Gaussen in *Percy, Prelate and Poet*,
in 1908.
2 The date is conjectural. A period closely following the preceding note is indicated by the fact that the two are identical
in appearance, written on paper of the same size, with the same
water-mark, "VI," folded and sealed identically, and addressed corner-wise, in a fashion not observed elsewhere
among his letters. Mrs Percy's absence from the Easton Maudit
vicarage, indicated in the note, also helps to fix its date during
the period of her attendance as wet-nurse upon the young prince.
3 The Percys' five children were left there.
4 He had probably started to compile his *Roman History* at this time.

you or Mrs. Percy? And when will you want to
be down yourselves?

I am your faithful friend

OLIVER GOLDSMITH

XXIII

To the Party at DR. BAKER'S¹

[London ? May, 1769]²

This *is* a poem! This *is* a copy of verses!³
Your mandate I got,
You may all go to pot;

1 From Prior's *Miscellaneous Works of Goldsmith*, IV, 1837, where
it was first published by permission of Major-General Sir Henry
Bunbury, Bart., the son of Catherine Bunbury. Although it
seems to be addressed to the whole group, it was appropriated
by the Hornecks, and was preserved at the Bunburys' seat at
Barton until late in the nineteenth century.

2 The date is conjectural and uncertain. It is contingent on the
date of the *Advertiser's* compliment, mentioned in the last line,
which, according to Prior, read as follows:

> While fair Angelica, with matchless grace,
> Paints Conwao's lovely form and Stanhope's face;
> Our hearts to beauty willing homage pay,
> We praise, admire, and gaze our souls away.
> But when the likeness she hath done for thee,
> O Reynolds! with astonishment we see,
> Forced to submit, with all our pride we own,
> Such strength, such harmony, excell'd by none,
> And thou art rivall'd by thyself alone.

Forster definitely states that these lines appeared on the same
day that the advertisement for the *Roman History* was published,
which was May 18. A search of the files of the *Public Advertiser*
fails to confirm this.

3 Evidently in reply to a demand for "a poem, a copy of verses"
from the Horneck sisters.

Had your senses been right,
You'd have sent before night;
As I hope to be saved,
I put off being shaved;
For I could not make bold,
While the matter was cold,
To meddle in suds,
Or to put on my duds;
So tell Horneck[1] and Nesbitt[2],
And Baker[3] and his bit,
And Kauffman[4] beside,
And the Jessamy bride[5],
With the rest of the crew,
The Reynoldses two[6],

[1] Mrs Hannah Horneck, mother of Mary and Catherine Horneck.
[2] Mr Nesbitt, the brother-in-law of Mr Thrale.
[3] Dr, afterwards Sir, George Baker (1722–1809), Reynolds' physician and intimate friend.
[4] Angelica Kauffmann (1741–1807), the most celebrated woman artist of the eighteenth century, who shared with Mary Moser the distinction of being the only women ever elected to the Royal Academy. She was a Swiss by birth, came to London in 1766, and achieved instant popularity. On November 22, 1767, she contracted a disastrous marriage with an impostor calling himself Count Horn, which was dissolved by a deed of separation dated February 10, 1768.
[5] Mary, the elder of the two beautiful Horneck sisters. She was not actually a bride until she married Colonel F. E. Gwyn in 1779.
[6] Joshua Reynolds and his sister, Miss Frances Reynolds.

Little Comedy's[1] face,
And the Captain in lace[2].
(By the bye you may tell him,
I have something to sell him;
Of use I insist,
When he comes to enlist.
Your worships must know
That a few days ago,
An order went out,
For the foot guards so stout
To wear tails in high taste,
Twelve inches at least;
Now I've got him a scale
To measure each tail,
To lengthen a short tail,
And a long one to curtail.)—
    Yet how can I when vext,
Thus stray from my text?
Tell each other to rue
Your Devonshire crew,
For sending so late
To one of my state.
But 'tis Reynolds's way
From wisdom to stray,
And Angelica's whim
To be frolic like him,

1 Catherine Horneck (–1799), the younger sister, who became
Mrs Henry William Bunbury in August, 1771.
2 Charles Horneck (–1804), the brother, who had purchased
an ensignship in the third regiment of Footguards on March 26,
1768.

But, alas! your good worships, how could they be
wiser,
When both have been spoil'd in to-day's Advertiser?   OLIVER GOLDSMITH

Here should appear GOLDSMITH'S *letter to* JAMES
BOSWELL, *written on September 21 or 22, 1769, inviting
him to meet* SIR JOSHUA REYNOLDS. *This letter is not
yet available for publication.*

XXIV

To MAURICE GOLDSMITH[1]

Dear Brother,   [London, *c.* January 10, 1770][2]

I should have answered your letter sooner,
but in truth I am not very fond of thinking of the
necessities of those I love when it is so very little
in my power to help them[3]. I am sorry to find
you are still every way unprovided for, and what
adds to my uneasiness is that I received a letter
from My Sister Johnson by which I learn that she
is pretty much in the same circumstances. As to
myself I believe I might get both you and my poor

1 From the original in the collection of Miss Constance Meade.
  It is addressed, "To Mr. Maurice Goldsmith at Mr. James
  Lawder's at Kilmore near Carrick on Shannon. Ireland." It
  was first published by Percy, in his Memoir, in 1801.
2 The date is determined by the postmark, "10 IA."
3 For the improbability of this, see § 1 of the Introduction.

brother in law something like that which you desire, but I am determined never to ask for little things or exhaust any little interest I may have untill I can serve you him and myself more effectually. As yet no opportunity has offered, but I believe you are pretty well convincd that I will not be remiss when it arrives. The King has been lately pleasd to make me Professor of ancient history[1] in a Royal Accademy of Painting which he has just establishd, but there is no sallary anex'd and I took it rather as a compliment to the institution than any benefit to myself. Honours to one in my situation are something like ruffles to a man that wants a shirt[2]. You tell me that there are fourteen or fifteen pound left me in the hands of my Cousin Lawder, and you ask me what I would have done with it? My dear Brother I would by no means give any directions to my dear worthy relations at Kilmore how to dispose of money that is more properly speaking theirs than mine. All that I can say is that I entirely,

---

1 One of the four honorary positions, which carried with them only the privilege of attending the meetings and the annual dinner. Dr Johnson was appointed Professor of Ancient Literature, Dr Francklin, of Cambridge, Chaplain, and Richard Dalton, the King's librarian, Antiquarian.

2 Cf. *The Haunch of Venison*, 1, 34: "It's like sending them ruffles, when wanting a shirt." Forster points out that this is borrowed from Tom Brown's *Laconics*: "To treat a poor wretch with a bottle of Burgundy...is like giving a pair of lace ruffles to a man that has never a shirt on his back."

and this letter will serve to witness give up any right or title to it[1], and I am sure they will dispose of it to the best advantage. To them I entirely leave it, whether they or you may think the whole necessary to fit you out, or whether our poor sister Johnson may not want the half I leave entirely to their and your discretion. The kindness of that good couple to our poor shattered family demands our sincerest gratitude, and tho' they have almost forgot me yet If good things at last arrive I hope one day to return and encrease their good humour by adding to my own. I have sent my cousin Jenny a miniature picture[2] of myself, as I believe it is the most acceptable present I can

1 Maurice's receipt for this transferred legacy is written on the back of the first page:

Received from Jam^s Lawder Esqr fifteen pounds Sterl. ye which sum is in full of a Legacy bequeathed to my Brother Oliver Goldsmith by ye last will and Testament of ye Revd Mr Tho. Contrine I say received ye same by Virtue of ye within power given to me by my s^d Brother Oliver Goldsmith. Wittness my hand this twenty fourth day of February 1770 seventy.

Maurice Goldsmith.

Wittness present
   Will: Hodson.

13 Gu^e	14	15	9
change		4	3
	15	0	0

For Maurice's use of this legacy, see § 1 of the Introduction.

2 The miniature has probably not survived. Austin Dobson (*Goldsmith's Poetical Works*, p. 261) thought it might be the original of the portrait engraved by Cook for Evans' edition of the *Poetical and Dramatic Works* or the painting engraved by Ridley.

85

offer. I have ordered it to be left for her at George Faulkener's[1] folded in a letter. The face you well know is ugly enough but it is finely painted. I will shortly also send my friends near the Shannon some Metzotinto prints[2] of myself[3], and some more of my friends here such as Burke[4], Johnson[5], Reynolds[6] and Coleman[7]. I believe I have written an hundred letters to different friends in your country and never received an answer from

1 The celebrated Dublin printer, George Faulkener.
2 The fashion, and the price, of mezzotint portraits received particular impetus in this year. Walpole, writing to Sir Horace Mann in May, said: "Another rage is for prints of English portraits. I have been collecting them for thirty years, and originally never gave for a mezzotint above one or two shillings. The lowest now are a crown; most from half a guinea to a guinea." The public exhibitions of the Royal Academy, started in 1769, were largely responsible for this increase of interest. The originals of three of the prints mentioned here, Goldsmith's own portrait, Johnson's, and Colman's, were hung together at the Royal Academy exhibit in the following April.
3 Engraved in 1770 by Giuseppe Filippo Liberati Marchi, Reynolds' protégé, from Reynolds' portrait, hung in the Royal Academy exhibit in this year.
4 No 1770 print of Burke seems to be known. Reynolds' portrait of him made in 1769 was engraved in 1771 by Watson.
5 Engraved by Watson in 1770, from Reynolds' portrait, hung in the Royal Academy exhibit of this year.
6 Engraved by Watson in 1770, from one of the four self-portraits which Reynolds made in 1769, a half-length, showing him with a cloak thrown over his shoulder, and his right hand in a portfolio.
7 No 1770 print of Colman seems to be known. Reynolds' portrait of him, exhibited at the Royal Academy in this year, was not engraved until 1773, when it was done by Marchi.

86

any of them. I dont know how to account for this, or why they are unwilling to keep up for me those regards which I must ever retain for them. If then you have a mind to oblige me you will write often whether I answer you or not. Let me particularly have the news of our family and old acquaintances. For instance you may begin by telling me about the family where you reside how they spend their time and whether they ever make mention of me. Tell me about my mother. My Brother Hodson, and his son, my brother Harry's son and daughter[1], My Sister Johnson, The family of Bally Oughter[2] what is become of them where they live and how they do. You talked of being my only Brother. I dont understand you. Where is Charles[3]? A sheet of paper occasionally filld with news of this kind would make me very happy, and would keep you nearer my mind. As it is my dear Brother believe me to be yours most affectionately

OLIVER GOLDSMITH

[1] Henry and Catherine Goldsmith;
[2] The family of his uncle, John Goldsmith.
[3] See § 1 of the Introduction for the bearing of this letter on the history of Charles.

XXV

To DR. WILLIAM HUNTER[1]

[London, *c.* June, 1770]

Dear Sir,

The young gentleman who carries this is my nephew. He has been liberally bred and has read something of physic and surgery, but desires to take the shortest and best method of being made more perfect in those studies. I beg sir you will put him in the way of improvement, and while he will take care to satisfy his instructors, I shall think my self laid under a particular obligation by your services or advice.

I am

Dear Sir

Your very humble serv't

OLIVER GOLDSMITH

[1] From the original in the possession of the Royal College of Surgeons of England, never before published. This is the letter to which Goldsmith refers in the following letter to his brother-in-law, *q.v.* It is dated conjecturally on the same grounds as the following letter.

XXVI

To DANIEL HODSON[1]

My dear Brother, [London, *c*. June, 1770][2]

I have the pleasure of informing you that your son William[3] is arrived in London in safety and joins with me in his kindest love and duty to you. Nothing gives me greater pleasure than the prospect I have of his behaving in the best and most dutiful manner both to you and the rest of the family. Sincerely I am charmed with his disposition and I am sure he feels all the good nature he expresses every moment for his friends at home. He had when he came here some thoughts of going upon the stage; I dont know where he could have contracted so beggarly an affection[4], but I have turned him from it and he is now sincerely bent on pursuing the study of physic

1 From Austin Dobson's *Life of Goldsmith*, where it was first published in 1888. It was called to Dobson's attention after his book was in the press, and was printed, along with Letters xxxi and xxxix, in an appendix, without comment.

2 The date is conjectural. It must fall approximately a twelvemonth before Letter xxxi, and must allow sufficient time after the preceding letter to Maurice for a second exchange of letters between Maurice and Oliver, and for Maurice's visit.

3 For this visit of William Hodson to London, see § 1 of the Introduction.

4 Goldsmith, however, numbered Garrick, the Yateses, Shuter, and other professional actors, among his personal friends. Johnson, also, held the profession in contempt while esteeming individual members of it.

89

and surgery in which he has already made a considerable progress and to which I have very warmly exhorted him. He will in less than a year be a very good Surgeon and he will understand a competent share of physic also. when he is fit for any business or any practice I shall use all my little interest in his favour. As for the stage it was every way a wild scheme and he is beside utterly unfit to succeed upon it. But while he is fitting himself for other business my dear Brother it is not proper that he should be utterly neglected. I have endeavoured to answer for you and my sister that some little thing should be done for him either here or at Edinburgh, and for my own part I am willing to contribute something towards his education myself. I believe an hundred pounds for a year or two would very completely do the business, when once he has got a profession he then may be thrown into any place with a prospect of succeeding. My Dear Dan think of this for a little, something *must* be done. I will give him twenty pounds a year, he has already about twenty more, the rest must be got, and your own good sense will suggest the means. I have often told you and tell you again that we have all good prospects before us, so that a little perseverance will bring things at last to bear. My brother Maurice was with me in London but it was not in my power to serve him effectually then[1]; indeed in a letter

1 See § 1 of the Introduction.

I wrote him I desired him by no means to come up but he was probably fond of the journey. I have already written to Dr. Hunter[1] in William's favour, and have got him cloaths, etc. I only wait your answer in what manner further to proceed and with the sincerest affection to you and my sister I am Dear Dan your most affectionate

Brother

OLIVER GOLDSMITH

I had a letter from Charles who is as he tells me possessed of a competency and settled in Jamaica[2].

XXVII

To SIR JOSHUA REYNOLDS[3]

My dear Friend,   [Lisle, *c.* July 27, 1770][4]

We had a very quick passage from Dover to Calais which we performed in three hours and

1 Dr William Hunter (1718–83), one of the leading physicians of the day. He was appointed first professor of anatomy in the Royal Academy in 1768.

2 See § 1 of the Introduction.

3 From an exact transcript of the original in the possession of Miss Constance Meade. It has no address. It was first published by Percy, in his Memoir, in 1801. Percy secured it from Boswell, who in turn had it from Reynolds, as is shown by a note in the margin, which reads, "Original letter of Dr. Goldsmith to Sir Joshua Reynolds, who gave it to me. James Boswell."

4 This is obviously the letter started at Lisle, and thrown aside, as too dull to send, which Goldsmith mentions in the following

twenty minutes, all of us extremely sea-sick, which must necessarily have happened as my machine to prevent sea-sickness was not completed. We were glad to leave Dover, because we hated to be imposed upon, so were in high spirits at coming to Calais where we were told that a little money would go a great way. Upon landing two little trunks, which was all we carried with us We were surprised to see fourteen or fifteen fellows all running down to the ship to lay their hands upon them, four got under each trunk, the rest surrounded and held the hasps, and in this manner our little baggage was conducted with a kind of funeral solemnity till it was safely lodged at the custom house. We were well enough pleased with the peoples civility till they came to be paid; every creature that had the happiness of but touching our trunks with their finger expected six-pence, and they had so pretty civil a manner of demanding it that there was no refusing them. When we had done with the porters, we had next, to speak with the custom house officers, who had

letter. The unfinished and unaddressed state of the letter is accounted for by this circumstance. It was evidently rescued by one of the Horneck ladies, with whom he was travelling, and sent to Reynolds. The biographers have assumed that it was written at Calais, but in that case there would have been no occasion for the letter started at Lisle, "giving a description of all that we have done and seen."

The date is conjectured from the fact that the trip from Lisle to Paris took two days by post.

their pretty civil way too. We were directed to
the Hotel d'Angleterre¹ where a valet de place
came to offer his service and spoke to me ten
minutes before I once found out that he was
speaking English. We had no occasion for his
service so we gave him a little money because he
spoke English and because he wanted it. I can't
help mentioning another circumstance,̓ [   ]²
bought a new ribbon for my wig at Canterbury,
and the barber at Calais broke it in order to gain
six-pence by buying me a new one.

XXVIII

To SIR JOSHUA REYNOLDS³

Paris July 29ᵗʰ [1770]

My Dear Friend.

I began a long letter⁴ to you from Lisle giving
a description of all that we had done and seen but
finding it very dull and knowing that you would

1 The hotel made famous by Sterne in *A Sentimental Journey*, in
  1768.
2 A name is blotted out in the MS. at this point, probably
  "Mary."
3 From the original in the collection of Mr W. M. Elkins, of
  Philadelphia. It is addressed: "To Sir Joshua Reynolds,
  Leicester Fields, London." It was first published by Prior, in
  his *Life*, in 1837.
4 See Letter xxvii, note 4.

shew it again I threw it aside and it was lost. You see by the top of this letter that we are at Paris, and (as I have often heard you say) we have brought our own amusement with us for the Ladies do not seem to be very fond of what we have yet seen. With regard to myself I find that travelling at twenty and at forty are very different things, I set out with all my confirmd habits about me and can find nothing on the continent so good as when I formerly left it. One of our chief amusements here is scolding at every thing we meet with and praising every thing and every person we left at home. You may judge therefore whether your name is not frequently bandied at table among us. To tell you the truth I never thought I could regret your absence so much as our various mortifications on the road have often taught me to do. I could tell you of disasters and adventures without number, of our lying in barns, and of my being half poisoned with a dish of green peas, of our quarelling with postillions and being cheated by Landladies but I reserve all this for an happy hour which I expect to share with you upon my return[1] I have very little to tell you more but that we are at present all well and expect

[1] It was a habit of their intimate friendship to visit together immediately upon the return of either from a journey. Upon Reynolds' return from Paris on October 23, 1768, they dined together on the two succeeding nights, and again upon his return in September, 1771.

returning when we have staid out our month, which I did not care tho it were over this very day. I long to hear from you all, how you yourself do, how Johnson, Burke, Dyer[1], Chamier[2], Colman, and every one of the club do. I wish I could send you some amusement in this letter but I protest I am so stupefied by the air of this country (for I am sure it can never be natural) that I have not a word to say. I have been thinking of the plot of a comedy which shall be entituled a journey to Paris, in which a family shall be introduced with a full intention of going to France to save money. You know there is not a place in the world more promising for that purpose. As for the meat of this country I can scarce eat it, and tho we pay two good shillings an head for our dinner I find it all so tough that I have spent less time with my knife than my pick tooth. I said this as a good thing at table but it was not understood. I believe it to be a good thing. As for our intended journey to Devonshire[3] I find it out of my power to perform it, for as soon as I arrive at Dover I intend to let the ladies go on, and I will take a country lodging for a couple of months somewhere near that place in order to do some

1 Samuel Dyer (1725–72), an intimate friend of Johnson's, and an early member of the Club.
2 Anthony Chamier (1725–80), then a secretary in the war office, and an original member of the Club.
3 Reynolds took the trip alone, setting out on September 7.

business[1]. I have so out run the constable that I must mortify a little to bring it up again. For Godsake the night you receive this take your pen in your hand, and tell me some thing about yourself, and my self if you know of anything that has happened. About Miss Reynolds, about Mr. Bickerstaff[2], my Nephew, or any body that you regard. I beg you will send to Griffin[3] the Book seller to know if there be any letters left for me and be so good as to send them to me at Paris. They may perhaps be left for me at the Porters Lodge opposite the Pump in Temple lane. The same messenger will do. I expect one from Lord Clare[4] from Ireland. As for others[5] I am not much

1 The work on his conscience was the *Animated Nature*, for the first five volumes of which Griffin had paid him in the September of the previous year, and the *History of England*, which he had contracted to finish for Davies by June, 1771.

2 Isaac Bickerstaffe (*c.* 1735–*c.* 1812), a talented young Irishman who had written *The Maid of the Mill* and other successful plays. His career ended in 1772, when he was charged with a capital crime of a depraved nature, and was judged to have admitted his guilt by flight. Since then, his connection with the great names of his day has been minimized, but he was certainly on intimate terms with Goldsmith, Reynolds, Garrick, and others. See also Letter XXXVI.

3 Griffin was publishing Goldsmith's *Deserted Village* at this time. It went into a fifth edition in August.

4 Robert Nugent (1702–88), of an old Westmeath family, elevated to the peerage in 1766 as Viscount Clare for his services in supporting the administration's taxation policy, was Goldsmith's staunch friend and patron.

5 It is supposed that the news of Goldsmith's mother's death was contained in this packet of letters, and that for this reason he

uneasy about. Is there any thing I can do for you at Paris, I wish you would tell me. The whole of my own purchases here is ·one silk coat which I have put on and which makes me look like a fool. But no more of that. I find that Colman has gaind his law suit[1]. I am glad of it. I suppose you often meet. I will soon be among you, better pleasd with my situation at home than I ever was before. And yet I must say that if any thing could make France pleasant the very good women with whom I am at present would certainly do it. I could say more about that but I intend shewing them this letter before I send it away. What signifies teizing you longer with moral observations when the business of my writing is over, I have one thing only more to say, and of that I think every hour in the day namely that I am your most   sincere and most affectionate friend

OLIVER GOLDSMITH

Direct to me at the Hotel de Denemarcs[2] Rue Jacob. Fauxbourg St Germains.

came directly back to London, abandoning his intended retreat near Dover.

1 The lawsuit was brought against Colman by his partners, Rutherford and Harris, for alleged refusal to consult them in managing the affairs of Covent Garden. In the public trial, Colman's acceptance of *The Good-Natured Man* without the partners' consent was cited as evidence against him.

2 Listed in the *Gentleman's Guide* as "Hotel de Dannemark, rue Jacob."

XXIX

To DOCTOR MACKENZIE[1]

[London, 1771 or 1772][2]

Doctor Goldsmith presents his compliments to Doctor Mackenzie, he will be at home this day till three, or at any other time the Doctor shall appoint. Or he will wait upon him, at Southwark.

He is engaged to dinner every day for this six or seven days.

XXX

To GEORGE AUGUSTUS SELWYN[3]

Sir,   Monday, April 15th, 1771

I did myself the honour of calling at your house in Chesterfield Street to deliver the enclosed, but not finding you at home and not knowing when you intend to return I take leave to inform you

1 From the original in the collection of Miss Constance Meade, never before published. The identity of Dr Mackenzie, or the letter's history before it reached Percy's hands, is not known.

2 The date is conjectural. The only clue is the watermark, SP, which is the same as that of the MS. sheets of *Animated Nature*, in the Mead collection, written in or near the year 1772. Dr Mackenzie's invitation, also in the Mead collection, reads,

Monday 10 [month indistinguishable]

"Dr. Mackenzie presents his compliments to Dr. Goldsmith. Begs he will let him know when he can have the pleasure of seeing him."

3 From a transcript of the original in volume five of the Selwyn correspondence, bequeathed by Mrs Cely-Trevilian to the Society of Antiquaries of London, never before published. It

98

that Colonel Nugent[1] entreats you will remember
your promise of putting Lord Marsh[2] in mind of
sending the tickets for the next Masquerade to me,
or sending what they call checque tickets which
will answer the same purpose. I entreat Sir you
will not impute this to my own impatience but that
of some finer people who if disappointed on this
occasion will be quite unhappy. Be pleased to
direct to Oliver Goldsmith at his chambers in The
Temple Brick Court No. 2. I am Sir your

most obedient humble Servant

OLIVER GOLDSMITH

XXXI

To DANIEL HODSON[3]

My dear Brother,   [London, *c*. June, 1771][4]

It gave me great concern to find that you
were uneasy at your son's going abroad. I will

is addressed, "To George Augustus Selwyn Esqr, Newmarket,
Cambridgeshire."
    Selwyn (1719–91) was a famous wit and politician, and a
leader at White's.

1 Son of Lord Clare. See p. 100, note 1.
2 So Goldsmith spells the name, although he probably refers to
    William Douglas (1724–1810), third earl of March and, later,
    fourth duke of Queensberry, known as "old Q," who was a
    close friend of Selwyn's, and also a member of White's.
3 From Dobson's *Life of Goldsmith*, where it was first published, in
    1888.
4 The dating is conjectural. It is determined approximately by
    the death of Colonel Nugent, referred to in the letter, which

99

7-2

beg leave to state my part in the affair and I hope
you will not condemn me for what I have endeavoured to do for his benefit. When he came
here first I learned that his circumstances were
very indifferent, and that something was to be
done to retrieve them. The stage was an abomin-
able resource which neither became a man of
honour, nor a man of sense. I therefore dissuaded
him from that design and turned him to physic
in which he had before made a very great progress,
and since that he has for this last twelve months
applied himself to surgery, so that I am thoroughly
convinced that there is not a better surgeon in the
kingdom of Ireland than he. I was obliged to go
down to Bath with a friend[1] that was dying when

took place at Bath on April 26 (*Gentleman's Magazine*, May,
1771). Since that time, as this letter makes clear, an exchange of
letters between William Hodson and his father had taken place.
1 The Hon. Lieut.-Colonel Nugent, only son of Lord Clare, must
be the person referred to. The biographers have noted Goldsmith's particular intimacy with Lord Clare in the spring and
summer of 1771, during his mourning for his son, but it has not
been previously known that Goldsmith was so intimately concerned with the son's death. The trip to Bath occurred after
April 23, when Goldsmith was present at the first annual dinner
of the Royal Academy, on which occasion he informed Walpole
of the death of Chatterton. Lord Hardwicke, who attended the
dinner, on the next day wrote Goldsmith a letter, preserved in
the British Museum, advising him to visit Bristol on his projected trip to Bath, and to recover such MSS. of Chatterton as
were available. This must have been the occasion, recorded in the
European Magazine (XXI, 88), of Goldsmith's unsuccessful attempt
to purchase the Rowley MSS. from George Catcott, of Bristol.

my nephew sent me down your letter to him in
which you inform him that he can no longer have
any expectations from you and that therefore he
must think of providing for himself. With this
letter he sent me one of his own where he asserted
his fixed intentions of going surgeon's mate to
India. Upon reading the two letters I own I
thought something was to be done. I therefore
wrote to a friend[1] in Town who procured him the
assurance of a place as full surgeon to India. This
with supplying him with about five and forty
pounds is what I did in my endeavours to serve
him. I thought him helpless and unprovided for,
and I was ardent in my endeavours to remove
his perplexities. Whatever his friends at home
may think of a surgeon's place to the East Indies,
it is not so contemptible a thing, and those who
go seldom fail of making a moderate fortune in
two or three voyages. But be this as it may
William is now prevailed upon to return home to
take your further advice and instructions upon
the matter. He has laboured very hard since he
left you, and is capable of living like a gentleman
in any part of the world. He has answered his
examinations as a Surgeon and has been found
sufficiently qualified. I entreat therefore you will
receive him as becomes him and you, and that
you will endeavour to serve the young man

1 Possibly Reynolds, who was a heavy stock-holder in the East
India Company, and a friend of William Hodson beside.

effectually not by foolish fond caresses but by
either advancing him in his business or setling
him in life. I could my Dear Brother say a great
deal more, but am obliged to hasten this letter
as I am again just setting out for Bath, and I
honestly say I had much rather it had been for
Ireland with my nephew, but that pleasure
I hope to have before I die.

I am Dear Dan
Your most affectionate
Brother OLIVER GOLDSMITH

XXXII

To BENNET LANGTON[1]

My Dear Sir

Since I had the pleasure of seeing you last
I have been almost wholly in the country at a

[1] From the original in the collection of Miss Constance Meade.
It is addressed, "To Bennet Langton Esq: at Langton near
Spilsby Lincolnshire." It was given by Langton to Percy, and
was first published by him, in his Memoir, in 1801. Langton's
invitation, to which this is a reply, is also preserved in Miss
Meade's collection, having evidently formed part of the packet
of letters turned over by Goldsmith to Percy in 1773. It reads:

Sep: 4th 1771
My dear Sir,

You was so kind, when I had the Pleasure of seeing you in
Town, as to speak of having Thoughts of giving me your
Company here. I wish very much you would put your kind

102

farmer's house¹ quite alone trying to write a
Comedy². It is now finished but when or how it
will be acted, or whether it will be acted at all are
questions I cannot resolve. I am therefore so much
employd upon that that I am under a necessity of
putting off my intended visit to Lincolnshire for
this season. Reynolds is just returned from Paris
and finds himself now in the case of a truant that
must make up for his idle time by diligence³. We

intention in Execution, in which Lady Rothes, who desires
Her best Compliments, very sincerely concurs with me—it was,
if you remember, at Sr Joshua Reynolds's that we talked of this,
who gave me Hopes too of letting us see Him. I would have
wrote to Him likewise to request that Favour, but in the Papers
it was said that he went to France some time ago, and I do not
know whether he is yet returned; if He is, and You have an
opportunity of seeing Him, will You be so kind as to mention
what I have said, and how much we wish for the Pleasure of
His Company—I have sent for the History of England, but
have not yet receivd it—some short extracts yt I have already
seen have entertained me much. Let me have the Pleasure of
hearing from you, Dear Sir, as soon as you conveniently can
after you receive this, and then, if you are so good as to say you
are coming, I will immediately write you word of the particulars
of the Road to this place and Means of conveyance &c—Will
you give me Leave to ask in what Forwardness is the Natural
History, or whether you are about any other Work that you
chuse as yet to speak of? I hope *Poetry* takes up some of Your
attention—but I will intrude upon you no longer than to say
that I am, Dear Sir, with great Respect and Regard

Your obedient humble Servant

Bennet Langton.

My Direction is Langton near Spilsby Lincolnshire.

1 Farmer Selby's, at the six-mile stone, Edgeware Road.
2 *She Stoops to Conquer*. It was subsequently, of course, much
revised, and was not produced until a year and a half after this
date.
3 The only sittings recorded in Sir Joshua's notebooks for September of this year are: George White, model for Ugolino; Miss

have therefore agreed to postpone the affair till
next summer when we hope to have the honour
of waiting upon her Ladyship[1] and you and staying
double the time of our late intended visit. We
often meet, and never without remembering you.
I see Mr Beauclerc[2] very often both in town and
country. He is now going directly forward to
become a second Boyle. Deep in Chymistry and
Physics. Johnson[3] has been down upon a visit to
a country parson Doctor Taylor's[4] and is returned
to his old haunts at Mrs. Thrale's. Burke[5] is
a farmer en attendant a better place, but visiting
about too. Every soul is visiting about and merry
but myself. And that is hard too as I have been

Simmons; Mr. Hickey. He probably returned from Paris for
the marriage of Catherine Horneck to William Henry Bunbury,
on August 26, and Goldsmith must certainly have come in from
Farmer Selby's for the same occasion.

1 The Dowager Countess of Rothes, whom Langton had married
in the preceding year.

2 The Hon. Topham Beauclerk (1739–80), a brilliant dilettante,
was one of the original members of the Club, and a particular
friend of Langton's.

3 Johnson had started on a six weeks' trip to Staffordshire and
Derbyshire on June 20. After his return he wrote to Langton,
on August 29, excusing himself for having failed to visit him at
Langton, where it seems he was expected with Goldsmith and
Reynolds.

4 The Reverend John Taylor, Johnson's school-fellow, prebendary
of Westminster and rector of Bosworth, lived at Ashbourne in
Derbyshire, where Johnson frequently visited him.

5 Burke had purchased Gregories, near Beaconsfield, in 1768,
and was now seriously engaged in scientific agriculture, while
the Junius excitement raged in London.

104

trying these three months to do something to make people laugh. There have I been strolling about the hedges studying jests with a most tragical countenance. The natural History is about half finished and I will shortly finish the rest. God knows Im tired of this kind of finishing, which is but bungling work, and that not so much my fault as the fault of my scurvy circumstances. They begin to talk in town of the opposition's gaining ground, the cry of Liberty[1] is still as loud as ever. I have published or Davis[2] has published for me an Abridgement of the History of England[3] for which I have been a good deal abused in the newspapers for betraying the liberties of the people[4]. God knows I had no thoughts for or

1 Cf. the speech of the intoxicated Jeremy in *She Stoops to Conquer*, Act IV, "Please your honour, Liberty and Fleet Street forever: Though I'm but a servant I'm as good as another man."

2 *Sic.*

3 *The History of England from the Earliest Times to the Death of George II,* published on August 6 of this year, not to be confused with the *Abridgment of the English History*, made by Goldsmith in 1774, and published after his death. Goldsmith regarded this present work as an abridgement from Hume, Carte, Rapin, and Smollett.

4 The passage which aroused especial censure was, according to Prior, the account of the trial of Sir John Friend, in which Lord Chief Justice Holt is accused of influencing the jury to pronounce Friend guilty. Since this passage, as well as what precedes, is taken bodily from Smollett, it is not to be wondered at that Goldsmith was surprised at the criticism of his political sympathies which it aroused. The Preface to the *History* is, however, distinctly more partisan on the Tory side than this disclaimer indicates.

against liberty in my head. My whole aim being
to make up a book of a decent size that as Squire
Richard¹ says would do no harm to nobody. However they set me down as an arrant Tory and
consequently no honest man. When you come to
look at any part of it you'l say that I am a soure
Whig. God bless you, and with my most respectful
compliments to her Ladyship I remain dear Sir

Your most affectionate

humble Servant,

OLIVER GOLDSMITH

Temple Brick Court
Sep.ᵣ 7ᵗʰ 1771

XXXIII

To JOSEPH CRADOCK²

[London, December, 1771]³

Mr. Goldsmith presents his best respects to
Mr. Cradock, has sent him the Prologue, such as

1 Unidentified. Possibly Richard Burke, brother of Edmund.
2 From Cradock's *Literary and Miscellaneous Memoirs*, where it was
first published, in 1828. It is addressed, "For the Rt. Hon.
Lord Clare, (Mr Cradock,) Gosfield, Essex." Joseph Cradock
(1742–1826), a wealthy country gentleman of Leicestershire,
and a literary and musical dilettante, made Goldsmith's
acquaintance some time before 1771, according to his own
recollection at the Yates's home. The prologue referred to here
was for Cradock's first play, *Zobeide*, adapted from Voltaire's
Les Scythes, especially for Cradock's friend, Mrs Yates.
3 The play was performed on December 10, 1771, at Covent
Garden.

106

it is. He cannot take time to make it better. He begs he will give Mr. Yates[1] the proper instructions; and so, even so, he commits him to fortune and the public.

XXXIV

To JOSEPH CRADOCK[2]

[London, February 16, 1772][3]

Mr. Goldsmith's best respects to Mr. Craddock when he ask'd him to day he quite forgot an

[1] Quick actually spoke it, the transfer being explained by Cradock (*Memoirs*, I, 224) on the grounds that "a comic Prologue, by the husband, in the character of a Sailor, would have ill-suited with the lofty dignity of the first tragic actress."

[2] From the original, in the possession of Mr A. S. W. Rosenbach, of New York. It is addresssed, "To J. Craddock Esqr at the Hotel in Pall Mall." It was first published in Cradock's *Literary and Miscellaneous Memoirs*, in 1828. Cradock did not remember to what performance the note referred, but said that it "seems to refer to one of his earlier productions." This production was the *Threnodia Augustalis*, written to be performed in commemoration of the Princess Dowager of Wales, who died on February 8, 1772. The biographers of Goldsmith, with the exception of Forster, have erroneously connected this note with *She Stoops to Conquer*.

[3] The date is determined by the fact that there were only two Sundays between the date of the Princess Dowager's death, on Saturday, February 8, and the performance of the *Threnodia Augustalis*, on Thursday, February 20. The letter could obviously not have been written on the day after her death, and the 16th is therefore the only possible date. See also § 4 of the Introduction.

engagement[1] of about a weeks standing which
has been made purposely for him, he feels himself
quite uneasy at not being permitted to have his
instructions upon these parts where he must
necessarily be defective. He will have a rehearsal
on monday; when it Mr. Craddock would come,
and afterwards take a bit of mutton chop it would
add to his other obligations.
Sunday moring[2].

XXXV

To the Reverend RICHARD PENNICK[3]

[Edgeware Road, *c.* March 16, 1772][4]
Dear Sir,

    I know not what apology to make for troubling
you with this letter, but the consciousness of your
readiness to oblige when it lies in your power.
Without more preface, I was some time ago, when
in London, looking over the Catalogue of the
Harleian Manuscripts, and in the middle or about

1 For the nature of the engagement, see § 4 of the Introduction.
2 *Sic.*
3 From *Notes and Queries* (5, VII, 102), where it was first published by
Mr S. H. Harlowe, of St John's Wood. According to Mr Harlowe,
the MS. was endorsed by Pennick, "I sent Dr. G. the MS."
    The Rev. Richard Pennick was rector of Abinger in Surrey,
and of St John, Southwark. He was also keeper of the reading
room of the British Museum.
4 For the date, see note 2 of the following letter.

the middle of that large book, the title and the beginning of an old Saxon poem[1] struck me very much. I soon after desired our friend Doctor Percy[2] to look out for it and get it transcribed for me, but he tells me he can find no such poem as that I mentioned. However, the poem I am sure is there, and there is nothing I so much desire, here, in a little country retirement where I now am, as to have that poem transcribed by one of the servants of the museum, and I don't know any body who can get that done for me except yourself. The poem is in Saxon before the time of Chaucer, and is I think about the middle of the volume among the names of several other poems. The subject is a consolation against repining at distress in this life, or some such title. The poem begins with these words, which are expressed in the Catalogue,

"Lollai, Lollai, littel childe, why weppest tou so sore?"

If you would find it out and order it to be transcribed for me, I will consider it as a singular

1 The poem is listed in the *Catalogue of Harleian Manuscripts in the British Museum* (1808, vol. 1) under Codex 913, number 23, as, "A Poem upon the Sorrows, & deceitfulness of this World. Incip. 'Lollai, lollai, litil Child, whi wepistou so sore.'" Heuser's tudy of the poem (*Die Kildare-Gedichte*, Bonn, 1904) places it in the fourteenth century. Goldsmith, as is obvious, made no distinction between Saxon and Middle English.

2 This circumstance throws additional light upon Goldsmith's and Percy's dependence on each other's interest in early English poetry.

favour, and will take care that the clerk shall be
paid his demand. I once more ask pardon for
giving you this trouble, and am, Dear Sir, your
very

Humble Servant,

OLIVER GOLDSMITH

P.S. A letter directed to me at the Temple will
be received.

XXXVI

To the Reverend R I C H A R D   P E N N I C K[1]

Monday [, March 16, 1772][2]

Dear Sir

I thank you heartily for your kind attention,
for the poem, for your letter, and every thing.
You were so kind as to say would not think it

1 From the original in the library of Haverford College. It is
addressed, "To the Revd Mr. Pennick at the Museum," and
above, in a different hand, is written, "Dr. Goldsmith. No. 49."
2 The date is determined from the following circumstances:
Goldsmith did not take up his residence at Edgeware until the
summer of 1771, when Percy was at Alnwick, Percy not returning to London until October, after Goldsmith had returned to
town. The notes must therefore date from the following spring,
after Goldsmith had returned to Edgeware, and must fall
before June, when the flight of Bickerstaffe from London
occurred. Sir Joshua Reynolds' notebook for 1772, in the
possession of the Royal Academy, records an engagement with
Goldsmith on Sunday, March 22, which is evidently the dinner
engagement referred to in the note.

troublesome to step out of town to see me. Sir
Joshua Reynolds Mr. Bickerstaff and a friend or
two more will dine with me next Sunday at the
place where I am which is a little Farmer's house
about six miles from town, the Edgeware road.
If you come either in their company or alone
I will consider it as an additional obligation.

I am dear Sir,

Your's most aff^{tly}

OLIVER GOLDSMITH

An Answer would be kind.

The place I am in is at Farmer Selby's at the six
mile Stone Edgeware road.

XXXVII

To JOHN EYLES[1]

[Edgeware Road, late March, 1772][2]

Honest John.

Give Doctor Percy,

My History of Animals[3]. Which you will find among my books.

1 From the original in the collection of Miss Constance Meade. It was first published in Gaussen's *Percy, Prelate and Poet*, in 1908. John Eyles was Goldsmith's servant.

2 The date is indicated by the fact that the MS., which is the lower portion of a folio sheet, shows on the verso the subscribed date of the letter from which it was torn, "March 21, 1772." Percy's diary in the British Museum has the following entry for March 31, "Mrs. Percy and I went to see Dr. Goldsmith and dined with him, came home in the evening." It was possibly on this occasion that Percy carried him his book.

Miss Gaussen makes the mistake of referring the note to the occasion, some time in the following year, when Goldsmith, who was out of town, asked Percy and Cradock to correct his proofs (Cradock, *Memoirs*, IV, 285).

3 Goldsmith was writing *The History of Animated Nature*. The verso of the MS. contains, beside the date mentioned, a list of fish jotted down in Goldsmith's hand. The book asked for is obviously one of the authorities from which he was compiling.

XXXVIII

To the DUKE OF NORTHUMBERLAND[1]

Mr Goldsmith presents his most respectful compliments to the Duke of Northumberland, and as
his Grace was pleased to allow him the liberty, he
begs permission for a few friends some day next
week to see his Grac[e's cast]le[2] at Sion.

Temple. May 22^{d} 1772.

XXXIX

To THOMAS BOND[3]

Temple. Brick Court.
December 16 1772

Dear Sir,

I received your letter, inclosing a draft upon
Kerr and company which when due shall be

1 From the original in the collection of Miss Constance Meade,
never before published.
  The Duke was Percy's patron, and a friend of Goldsmith's.
Percy, who acted as the Duke's secretary, undoubtedly secured
this note directly from the Duke for the Memoir, but finding
it of small importance, omitted it.
2 Obliterated by the seal.
3 From Dobson's *Life of Goldsmith*, where it was first published,
in 1888. It is addressed, according to Dobson, "Mr. Thomas

applied to the discharge of a part of my nephew's debts. He has written to me from Bristol for ten pound which I have sent him in a bank note enclosed he has also drawn upon me by one Mr. Odonogh for ten pound more, the balance therefore having paid his servant maid[1], as likewise one or two trifles more remains with me. As he will certainly have immediate and pressing occasion for the rest when he arrives I beg youl remit the rest to me and I will take care to see it applied in the most proper manner. He has talked to me of a matrimonial scheme[2]. If that could take place all would soon be well. I am Dear Sir your affection Kinsman and humble servant

OLIVER GOLDSMITH

Be pleased to answer this directly.

Bond Attorney in Montrath Street Dublin." Bond is probably the "connection of the family by marriage," mentioned by Prior (I, 17), who purchased the estate of Lisoy from Henry Goldsmith's son, Henry, in 1802.

1 William Hodson kept a separate establishment at No. 41 Newman Street (Prior, II, 145).

2 The plan must have been abortive, since, according to Prior (II, 145), his first wife was a Miss Longworth, of Westmeath.

XL

To the Reverend THOMAS PERCY[1]

[London, 1772 or 1773][2]

Dear Sir

I wish you would write for me the names of such persons as have written papers in the Spectator[3], at the end of every paper belonging to Addison and Steel &c there are letters. There are some however which are without marks. Those

1 From the original in the collection of Miss Constance Meade, never before published. It is addressed, "To the Rev.ᵈ Doctor Percy."

2 The date is conjectured from the water-mark of the paper— "LVG"—familiar in Goldsmith's correspondence during 1772 and 1773, and unknown before September, 1771. The later period is made more probable by the fact that the letter of the publisher Wilson (see the next note) was included in the packet given to Percy by Goldsmith in 1773.

3 Goldsmith was preparing an edition of *The Spectator* for an Irish publisher, Wm Wilson. A letter from him to Goldsmith is described in the sales catalogue of Wm Evarts Benjamin, for March, 1886, as follows: "Mr. Wm. Wilson. Publisher. A.L.S. 1 p., 4to. n.d. To Dr. Goldsmith on his departure for Dublin, and wishes to know if the idea of an Irish edition of the *Spectator*, with the authors' names prefixed to the articles, meets with the Doctor's views, and also asks his terms for the work." The letter formed part of a group of letters which became detached from Percy's collection and were offered for sale together in this catalogue. No evidence that the edition ever appeared has been discovered.

names I wish to have. I have [sent]¹ you a little book where the numbers are mark'd, to which I beg you'l add the names.

Yours ever.

OLIVER GOLDSMITH

Ill call or send on Sunday morning, being constrain'd for time.

XLI

To GEORGE COLMAN²

[London, January, 1773]³

Dear Sir

I entreat you'l relieve me from that state of suspense in which I have been kept for a long time. Whatever objections you have made or shall make to my play I will endeavour to remove⁴ and not argue about them. To bring in any new judges either of its merits or faults I can never submit to. Upon a former occasion when my other play was before Mr. Garrick he offered to bring me before

---

1 "Sent" is inserted with a caret, in a different hand.
2 From *Posthumous Letters...addressed to...George Colman the Elder*, where it was first published, in 1820.
3 Prior's conjectural dating is retained.
4 For the alterations made by Goldsmith, see § 5 of the Introduction.

116

Mr. Whitehead's[1] tribunal but I refused the proposal with indignation: I hope I shall not experience as hard treatment from you as from him. I have as you know a large sum of money[2] to make up shortly; by accepting my play I can readily satisfy my Creditor that way, at any rate I must look about to some certainty to be prepared. For God sake take the play and let us make the best of it, and let me have the same measure at least which you have given as bad plays as mine.

I am your friend

and servant

OLIVER GOLDSMITH

XLII

To DAVID GARRICK[3]

[London, early February, 1773][4]

Dear Sir

I ask you many pardons for the trouble I gave you of yesterday. Upon more mature deliberation

1 The Poet Laureate.
2 The nature of this obligation is not known.
3 From the original in the possession of Mr A. Edward Newton, of Philadelphia. It is addressed, "To David Garrick Esqr. Adelphi," and is endorsed in Garrick's hand, "Dr. Goldsmith's about his play." It was first published in Boaden's *Correspondence of David Garrick*, vol. I.
4 The letter is definitely dated "February 6" in Boaden's *Correspondence*, but nothing on the MS. warrants the date.

and the advice of a sensible friend¹ I begin to
think it indelicate in me to throw upon you the
odium of confirming Mr. Colman's sentence.
I therefore request you will send my play by my
servant back, for having been assured of having
it acted at the other house, tho' I confess yours in
every respect more to my wish, yet it would be
folly in me to forego an advantage which lies in
my power of appealing from Mr. Colman's
opinion to the judgement of the town². I entreat,
if not too late, you will keep the affair a secret for
some time. I am Dear Sir

your very humble servant

OLIVER GOLDSMITH

XLIII

To JOSEPH CRADOCK³

[London, *c*. March 16, 1773]⁴
My dear Sir,

   The Play has met with a success much beyond
your expectations or mine. I thank you sincerely

1 Generally thought to have been Johnson.
2 Cf. *The Present State of Polite Learning*, chap. XI, "And this may
  be the reason why so many writers at present are apt to appeal
  from the tribunal of criticism to that of the people."
3 From Cradock's *Literary and Miscellaneous Memoirs*, where it was
  first published, in 1828.
4 The letter was written between the first performance of *She
  Stoops to Conquer*, on March 15, and the first benefit night, on
  March 18.

for your Epilogue[1], which, however, could not be used, but with your permission, shall be printed. The story in short is this; Murphy[2] sent me rather the outline of an Epilogue than an Epilogue, which was to be sung by Mrs. Catley[3], and which she approved. Mrs. Bulkley[4] hearing this, insisted on throwing up her part, unless, according to the custom of the theatre, she were permitted to speak the Epilogue. In this embarrassment I thought of making a quarelling Epilogue between Catley and her, debating who should speak the Epilogue, but then Mrs. Catley refused, after I had taken the trouble of drawing it out. I was then at a loss indeed; an Epilogue was to be made, and for none but Mrs. Bulkley. I made one, and Colman thought it too bad to be spoken; I was obliged therefore to try a fourth time, and I made a very mawkish thing, as you'll shortly see. Such is the history of my Stage adventures, and which I have at last done with. I cannot help saying, that I am very sick of the stage; and though I believe I shall get three tolerable benefits, yet I shall upon the

1 For a further account of this epilogue, as well as of the other epilogues mentioned in the letter, see § 5 of the Introduction.
2 Arthur Murphy (1727–1805), a playwright, was a compatriot and old friend of Goldsmith's, as well as a friend of Cradock's.
3 Anne Catley, a singer, made her début at Covent Garden in 1762, and remained with the company until 1784. The part of Miss Neville, for which she was cast, was actually taken in the performance by Mrs Kniveton, for unexplained reasons.
4 Mrs Bulkley, a niece of John Rich, made her first appearance on the stage as Miss Willford, in 1765.

whole be a loser, even in a pecuniary light[1]; my
ease and comfort I certainly lost while it was in
agitation.

I am, my dear Cradock,

your obliged, and obedient servant,

OLIVER GOLDSMITH

P.S. Present my most humble respects to Mrs.
Cradock.

XLIV

To the DUKE OF NORTHUMBERLAND[2]

Temple. Thursday March 18 [, 1773]

Doctor Goldsmith presents his most humble
respects to his Grace[3] with his sincere thanks for
his kind countenance and protection upon the
present occasion[4]. He will take care for his Graces
reception.

---

1 Goldsmith's actual profit from his three nights was, for the first
   night, £183. 10s. 0d., for the second, £171. 17s. 0d., and for the
   third, £147. 11s. 6d., making a total of £502. 18s. 6d. (*Covent
   Garden Ledger*, B.M. Eg. 2277).
2 From the original in the collection of Miss Constance Meade,
   never before published. It was evidently secured by Percy
   directly from the Duke, whose secretary he was. It is endorsed
   on the verso with red ink, in Percy's hand, "Goldsmith."
3 "Duke of North^d " is here inserted with a caret, in another hand.
4 The author's first benefit night of *She Stoops to Conquer*, on the
   day of this letter.

1773]   *To* MRS. THRALE

Here should appear GOLDSMITH'S *letter to* JAMES
BOSWELL, *written on April 4, 1773, in response to his
congratulations on the success of* SHE STOOPS TO CONQUER.
This letter is not yet available for publication.

XLV

To MRS. THRALE¹

[London, *c.* April 12, 1773]²

Madam

I ask a thousand pardons. I did not know what
were the volumes I sent, but sent what I had. Nor
did I know the volumes you wanted, for I knew
you had read some. I beg youl not impute it to
any thing but the strange dissipation of one who
hates to think of any thing like his duty. I will
take care tomorrow of the volumes in question,
and am Madam with the utmost respect and esteem

your humble serv!

OLIVER GOLDSMITH

1 From the original in the possession of Mr W. G. Panter, of
Dublin. It is addressed, "To Mrs. Thrale," and is endorsed
by her, "a Letter from Dr. Goldsmith." It was first published
in Broadley's *Doctor Johnson and Mrs. Thrale,* in 1910.
2 The date is determined by the date of Mrs Thrale's letter, to
which this is evidently a reply. This letter is described in the
sales catalogue of Wm Evarts Benjamin, for March, 1886, as
follows: "Hester L. Thrale (Mrs. Piozzi). 12th April 1773.
A.L.S. 1 p., 4to. To Doctor Goldsmith, urging him to let her
have the fourth and fifth volumes of his book (she does not say
which one), and couched in terms of much stately courtesy."
The title of the volumes referred to does not appear.

121

XLVI

To JOHN NOURSE[1]

[London, April 26, 1773][2]

Sir

The bearer is Dr Andrews[3] who has just finished a work relative to Denmark which I have seen, and read with great pleasure. He is of opinion that a short letter of this kind expressing my approbation will be a proper introduction of it to you; I therefore once more recommend it in the warmest manner, and unless I am mistaken, it will be a great credit to him, as well as of benefit to the purchaser of the copy.

I am Sir

Your most obedient Servt

OLIVER GOLDSMITH

1 From the original in the Dreer collection, belonging to the Pennsylvania Historical Society. It is addressed, "To Mr. Nourse," and is endorsed, in another hand, "Dr. Goldsmith April 26, 1773." It was first published by Prior, in 1837.

John Nourse (–1780), the publisher, brought out Goldsmith's *Animated Nature.*

2 The date of the endorsement.

3 John Andrews, LL.D. (1736–1809), author of *Letters to the Count de Wilderen*, 1781; *Inquiries into the Manners, Tastes, and Amusements of the two last Centuries in England*, 1782; *History of the War with America*, 1785, etc. The work mentioned here, *The History of the Revolutions of Denmark*, etc., which Nourse published in April, 1774, was his first publication, and, as Prior suggests, was probably written to satisfy the public interest aroused by Queen Matilda's misfortunes.

XLVII

To DAVID GARRICK[1]

Temple, June 10th, 1773[2]

Dear Sir,

To be thought of by you obliges me; to be served by you is still more. It makes me very happy to find that Dr. Burney thinks my scheme of a dictionary useful; still more that he will be so kind as to adorn it with any thing of his own. I beg you will also accept my gratitude for procuring me so valuable an acquisition.

I am, dear Sir,

Your most affectionate servant,

OLIVER GOLDSMITH

1 From Prior's *Life of Goldsmith*. It was first published by Mme D'Arblay, in *Memoirs of Dr Burney*, in 1832. Prior's version, which was secured from Mme D'Arblay on a visit to her in 1831, is preferred because it shows less evidence of correction.

The letter refers to Goldsmith's projected *Dictionary of the Arts and Sciences*, for which Garrick had induced Dr Burney to write the article on music. Garrick sent the letter to Burney on June 11, with the following note: "My dear Doctor, I have sent you a letter from Dr. Goldsmith. He is proud to have your name among the elect. Love to all your fair ones. Ever yours, D. Garrick." Young Fanny Burney was so much impressed by Goldsmith's letter that she copied it from memory into her diary.

2 So Prior. Mme D'Arblay dates it, "Jan. 10," evidently a misreading.

XLVIII

To THOMAS CADELL[1]

[London, 1773 or 1774][2]

Doctor Goldsmiths compliments to Mr. [Cadell,][3] and desires a set of the history of England for correction if interleaved the better[4].

1 From a transcript of the original in the Bodleian Library. It was first published by Prior, in his *Life*, in 1837.

  Thomas Cadell, publisher, brought out the second edition of Goldsmith's *History of England*, having purchased the copyright from the original owner, Davies.

2 The date is uncertain. The second edition of the *History*, which Goldsmith was preparing, was not announced for publication in the *London Chronicle* until December 15, 1774, more than eight months after Goldsmith's death. I am indebted to Mr R. W. Seitz for this information.

3 So the name appears in Prior's version. In the MS. as it now stands, the name is cut out, and on the mount on which it is laid down, the name "Nourse" was written in by Wm Upcott, to whom the MS. formerly belonged.

4 The end of the note is cut away.

XLIX

To THOMAS CADELL[1]

[London, 1773 or 1774]

Mr. Goldsmith's compliments to Mr. Cadell, begs for an hour or two the use of Millot's History by Mrs. Brooke[2].

L

To DAVID GARRICK[3]

[London, *c.* December 24, 1773][4]

My Dear Sir,

Your saying you would play my "Good-natured Man" makes me wish it[5]. The money you ad-

1 From the original in the possession of Mr A. S. W. Rosenbach, of New York. It was first published by Prior, in his *Life*, in 1837. It is addressed, very unevenly, "Mr. Cadell, Strand." It obviously follows the preceding note closely in point of time.

2 Claude-François-Xavier Millot (1726–85) wrote *Élémens de l'Histoire d'Angleterre depuis la conquête des Romains jusqu'au règne de George II* in 1769, and it was translated by Mrs Frances Brooke (1724–89) in 1770.

3 From Forster's *Life of Goldsmith*, where it was first published, in 1848. It is endorsed, according to Forster, "Goldsmith's parlaver," in Garrick's hand.

4 The date is determined by the date of the following letter, which it immediately precedes. Previous editors have dated this transaction from the late summer of 1773, or simply "1773," and have not connected it with the Christmas visit to Barton.

5 This proposal was never acted upon, probably because of Garrick's increasing ill-health.

vanced me upon Newbery's note[1] I have the mortification to find is not yet paid, but he says he will in two or three days. What I mean by this letter is to lend me sixty pound for which I will give you Newbery's note, so that the whole of my debt will be an hundred for which you shall have Newbery's note as a security. This may be paid either from my alteration if my benefit should come to so much, but at any rate I will take care you shall not be a loser. I will give you a new character in my comedy and knock out Lofty which does not do, and will make such other alterations as you direct.

I am yours

OLIVER GOLDSMITH

I beg an answer.

1 Nothing further is known of this note. Forster assumed that Garrick had held it since before September, 1771, and that it was unpaid because of "disputed claims on behalf of the elder Newbery's estate." Francis Newbery had, however, accepted the copyright of *She Stoops to Conquer* in satisfaction of all his claims on Goldsmith, who was, therefore, justified in resenting the delay in payment of this note.

LI

To DAVID GARRICK[1]

[London, December 25, 1773][2]

My Dear Friend

I thank you! I wish I could do something to serve you. I shall have a comedy[3] for you in a season or two at farthest that I believe will be worth your acceptance, for I fancy I will make it a fine thing. You shall have the refusal. I wish you would not take up Newbery's note, but let

1 From the facsimile reproduction of the original, in the catalogue of Mr R. B. Adam's library. It is endorsed, in Garrick's hand, "Goldsmith's Parlaver." It was first published by Prior, in his *Life*, in 1837.

2 The date is determined by the date of Goldsmith's note, which accompanied the letter. This note, which took the form of a bill of exchange, has survived, and now belongs to Mr A. S. W. Rosenbach. It was unknown to Prior and Forster, and was known to Cunningham and Gibbs only through a notice in a Sotheby catalogue in 1851, which gave the date simply as " 1773." The bill reads:

Sir, 28 Jany. £60 0 0 December 25th, 1773. One month after date pay the bearer the sum of sixty pounds and place it to the account of Sir your humble servant

Oliver Goldsmith.

To David Garrick Esqr
Adelphi.

It is signed at the foot, "Dec. 25, 1773 Accepted—D. Garrick," and on the back bears Goldsmith's signature, and those of Charles Ekerobh Mall, and Josiah Shaw, for B. St. Moyen Esqr. The date, " 28 Jany." is evidently the date of payment.

3 Nothing more is known of this projected comedy.

Waller¹ teize him, without however coming to extremities, let him haggle after him and he will get it. He owes it and will pay it. Im sorry you are ill. I will draw upon you one month after date for sixty pound, and your acceptance will be ready money part of which I want to go down to Barton² with. May God preserve my honest little man for he has my heart.

ever

OLIVER GOLDSMITH

LII

To MRS. BUNBURY³

Madam.   [London, *c.* December 25, 1773]⁴

I read your letter⁵ with all that allowance which critical candour would require, but after

1 Forster surmised that Goldsmith meant Wallis, Garrick's solicitor.
2 The family seat of the Bunburys. See the next letter.
3 From the original, in the Morgan Library, New York City. It was first published by Prior, in *Goldsmith's Miscellaneous Works*, in 1837. The address does not appear, but it is clearly written to Catherine Horneck Bunbury, in reply to an invitation written in the same vein. See note 3.
4 The date is definitely limited by the date of Garrick's loan (see the preceding letter, note 2) on which his visit was contingent. It could hardly have been written before the acceptance of the loan, on Friday, December 25, nor could it have been written later than Saturday, December 26, since Goldsmith speaks of his proposed New Year's visit as "some day next week." Prior and other editors dated the letter "1772," and Sir Henry Bunbury (*Correspondence of Sir Thomas Hanmer*) dated it "1773 or 1774."
5 Her letter is preserved in a contemporary copy, in a hand which

all find so much to object to, and so much to raise my indignation, that I cannot help giving it a serious reply. I am not so ignorant madam as not to see there are many sarcasms contain'd in it, and solœcisms also (solœcism is a word that comes from the town of Soleis[1] in Attica among the

bears a strong resemblance to Edmund Burke's, sold among a collection of letters by and to Bennet Langton, which now belongs to Mr W. M. Elkins of Philadelphia:

> I hope my good Doctor you soon will be here
> And your spring velvet coat very smart will appear
> To open our ball the first day of the year.
> And bring with you a wig that is modish and gay
> To dance with the girls that are makers of Hay;
> Tho of Hay we don't often hear talk in these times,
> Yet it serves very well towards making of rhimes.
> My sister will laugh at my rhimes about Hay,
> Yet this I am sure I may venture to say,
> That we all here do wish and intreat and desire
> You will straightway come hither and sit by our fire.
> And if you will like in the evening to game
> We'll all play at Loo where you'll surely get fame
> By winning our money away in a trice,
> As my sister and I will give you advice.
> Or if you would shoot, Sir, we'll lend you a gun,
> And Druid t'oblige will after Birds run.
> But if you like better to hunt o'er the ground[s]
> Mr. B[unbur]y'll lend you [so]me [ve]ry good Hounds.
> But these simple sports to a fine London Beau
> Who doubtless is thinking of fashion and show
> And whose interested friends all wish to detain,
> As they know very well what pleasure they gain
> By keeping one with them they so much admire
> And whose cheerful company always desire,
> Yet to leave these pleasures if he condescends
> He will greatly oblige his very good friends.

Goldsmith's reply alludes to this throughout.

1 The *New English Dictionary* gives the derivation from the town of Soloi, in Cilicia, Asia Minor, where a corrupt Attic dialect was spoken.

Greeks, built by Solon, and applied as we use the word kidderminster[1] for curtains from a town also of that name, but this is learning you have no taste for) I say madam there are sarcasms in it and solœcisms also. But not to seem an ill natured critic Ill take leave to quote your own words and give you my remarks upon them as they occur. You begin as follows,

I hope my good Doctor you soon will be here
And your spring velvet coat very smart will appear
To open our ball the first day in the year.

Pray madam where did you ever find the Epithet good applied to the title of Doctor? Had you calld me learned Doctor, or grave Doctor, or Noble Doctor it might be allowable because these belong to the profession. But not to cavil at triffles; you talk of my spring velvet coat and advise me to wear it the first day in the year, that is in the middle of winter. A spring velvet in the middle of winter?!! That would be a solœcism indeed. And yet to encrease the inconsistence, in another part of your letter you call me a beau. Now on one side or other you must be wrong. If Im a beau I can never think of wearing a spring velvet in winter, and if I be not a beau— why—— then—— that explains itself. But let me go on to your next two strange lines

1 A town in Worcestershire, famous for stuffs in which the pattern was woven into the material.

And bring with you a wig that is modish
    and gay
To dance with the girls that are makers
    of hay.

The absurdity of making hay at Christmass you
yourself seem sensible of. You say your sister will
laugh, and so indeed she well may—the lattins have
an expression for a contemptuous kind of laughter,
naso contemnere adunco[1] that is to laugh with a
crooked nose, she may laugh at you in the manner
of the ancients if she thinks fit. But now I come
to the most extraordinary of all extraordinary
propositions which is to take your and your
sister's advice in playing at Loo[2]. The presumption
of the offer raises my indignation beyond the
bounds of prose it inspires me at once with verse
and resentment. I take advice! And from who?
You shall hear.

First let me suppose what may shortly be true
The company set, and the word to be Loo.
All smirking, and pleasant, and big with adven-
    ture
And ogling the stake which is fixd in the center.

1 Dobson (*Goldsmith's Poems*, 1906) quotes Horace, Sat. 1, 6, 5:
"*naso suspendis adunco/Ignotos....*"
2 A round game played on the principle of whist, with trumps,
in which any number could participate, the object being to
take the pool by winning the largest number of tricks. There
were two kinds, three-card and five-card Loo, the latter being
evidently in favour at Barton.

Round and round go the cards while I inwardly
    damn
At never once finding a visit from Pam[1].
I[2] lay down my stake, apparently cool,
While the harpies about me all pocket the pool.
I fret in my gizzard, yet cautious and sly
I wish all my friends may be bolder than I.
Yet still they sit snugg, not a creature will aim
By losing their money to venture at fame[3].
Tis in vain that at niggardly caution I scold
Tis in vain that I flatter the brave and the bold
All play in their own way, and think me an ass.
What does Mrs. Bunbury? I sir? I pass.
Pray what does Miss Horneck?[4] Take courage.
    Come do.
Who I! Let me see sir. Why I must pass too.
Mr. Bunbury[5] frets, and I fret like the devil
To see them so cowardly lucky and civil.
Yet still I sit snugg and continue to sigh on
Till made by my losses as bold as a lion
I venture at all, while my avarice regards
The whole pool as my own. Come give me five cards.

1 The knave of clubs, which took precedence over the ace of
  trumps.
2 Two lines are crossed out here, which read, as far as they are
  decipherable, "I lay down my stake [   ] that too/While
  some harpy beside me picks up the whole—."
3 Cf. Mrs Bunbury's line, "We'll all play at Loo where you'll
  surely get fame."
4 Mary Horneck, the Jessamy Bride of Letter xxiii.
5 Henry Bunbury, Catherine Horneck's husband.

Well done cry the ladies. Ah Doctor that's good.
The pool's very rich. Ah. The Doctor is lood[1].
Thus foild in my courage, on all sides perplext,
I ask for advice from the lady that's next
Pray mam be so good as to give your advice
Dont you think the best way is to venture fort twice.
I advise cries the lady to try it I own.
Ah! The Doctor is lood. Come Doctor, put down.
Thus playing and playing I still grow more eager
And so bold and so bold, Im at last a bold beggar.
Now ladies I ask if law matters youre skilld in
Whether crimes such as yours should not come
    before Fielding[2]
For giving advice that is not worth a straw
May well be call'd picking of pockets in law
And picking of pockets with which I now charge ye
Is by Quinto Elizabeth[3] death without Clergy.
What justice when both to the Old Baily brought
By the gods Ill enjoy it, tho' 'tis but in thought.

1 The player who won no tricks was looed, and as a penalty had
  to forfeit the pool and contribute to the next pool.
2 Sir John Fielding, half-brother to Henry Fielding, whom he
  succeeded as justice of the peace for Westminster, on the latter's
  death in 1754.
3 The act referred to, as Dobson points out, is really Octavo
  Elizabeth, an act against "Cutpurses or Pyckpurses," condemn-
  ing them to "suffer Death in suche a maner and fourme as they
  shoulde if they were no Clarkes" (*Statutes of the Realme*, IV,
  chap. v, 1819). This familiarity with the law, the mistake notwithstanding, lends plausibility to the tradition that Goldsmith
  was at one time a candidate for the Gresham lectureship in civil
  law.

Both are placed at the bar with all proper decorum.
With bunches of Fennel and nosegays before em.[1]
Both cover their faces with mobbs[2] and all that
But the judge bids them angrily take of their hat.
When uncovered a buzz of enquiry runs round
Pray what are their crimes? They've been pilfer-
    ing found.
But pray who have they pilfered? A Doctor I hear.
What, yon solemn fac'd odd[3] looking man that
    stands near,
The same. What a pitty. How does it surprize one
Two handsomer culprits I never set eyes on.
Then their friends all come round me with cringing
    and leering
To melt me to pitty, and soften my swearing.
First Sir Charles[4] advances, with phrases well strung
Consider Dear Doctor the girls are but young.
The younger the worse I return him again.
It shews that their habits are all dy'd in grain.
But then theyre so handsome, one's bosom it
    grieves.
What signifies handsome when people are thieves.

1 "A practice dating from the gaol-fever of 1750" (Dobson's
  Life of Goldsmith, p. 168, note).
2 The ordinary morning head-dress of women in the early and
  middle eighteenth century.
3 Goldsmith first wrote, and crossed out,—"Yon handsome fac'd
  [sm]all" for "What, yon solemn fac'd odd".
4 Henry Bunbury's older brother, the owner of the family seat of
  Barton. The property descended to the son of Catherine and
  Henry Bunbury, who became Sir Henry Bunbury.

But where is your justice; their cases are hard.
What signifies justice; I want the reward.————

Theres the parish of Edmonton offers forty pound;
there's the parish of St Leonard Shoreditch offers
forty pound; there's the parish of Tyburn from
the hog in the pound to St Giles's watch house
offers forty pound, I shall have all that if I convict
them.

But consider their case, It may yet be your own
And see how they kneel; is your heart made of
    stone?
This moves, so at last I agree to relent
For ten pounds in hand, and ten pound to be
    spent.
The judge takes the hint, having seen what we
    drive at
And lets them both off with correction in private[1].

---

1 The couplet "The judge takes the hint...correction in private"
was omitted in Prior's and Bunbury's versions and is here
restored for the first time. A correspondent in the *Academy*
(xxvi, 342) noted that they were contained in a MS. copy of
the poem belonging in the Northcote papers now in the
Proprietary Library of Plymouth, but Gibbs rejected the
lines (*Academy*, xxvi, 377) because they did not appear in
Bunbury's version. The recovery of the original MS. resolves
all doubt on the question, but leaves unsettled Sir Henry's
reasons for excising the apparently harmless lines. That the
omission was intentional and not accidental seems to be proved
by another contemporary copy in the collection of Langton
papers previously referred to, belonging to Mr W. M. Elkins,
in which the two lines in question were first written and then
carefully scored out.

I chalenge you all to answer this. I tell you you cannot. It cuts deep. But now for the rest of the letter, and next—but I want room—so I believe I shall battle the rest out at Barton some day next week. I dont value you all.

LIII

To JOHN NOURSE[1]

[London, *c.* February 20, 1774][2]

Sir,

As the work for which we engaged is now near coming out[3] and for the *over* payment[4] of which I return you my thanks, I would consider myself still more obliged to you, if you would let my friend Griffin[5] have a part of it. He is ready to

1 From Prior's *Life of Goldsmith*, where it was first published, in 1837. John Nourse brought out Goldsmith's *Animated Nature*, to which this letter refers.

2 The date is supplied by the endorsement, which, according to Prior, is "February 20, 1774."

3 The *St James Chronicle* advertised it on February 5, 1774, "to be published next month," but it was not, as a matter of fact, issued until after Goldsmith's death, on June 30.

4 No record of this additional payment exists.

5 William Griffin, bookseller in Catherine Street in the Strand, and Goldsmith's particular friend. He was an Irishman himself and patron of the Irish men of letters in London. He originally contracted for the *Animated Nature* in 1769, and three days before paying Goldsmith five hundred guineas in advance for the first five volumes, on September 26, 1769, he sold half

pay you for any part you will think proper to give him, and as I have thoughts of extending the work into the *vegetable* and *fossil* kingdoms, you shall share with him in any such engagement as may happen to ensue.

I am Sir,

Your very humble servant,

OLIVER GOLDSMITH

the copyright to Nourse, probably, as Prior plausibly conjectures, to secure ready money for the payment to Goldsmith. Eventually the entire copy was sold to Nourse. Before the transfer of the entire property took place, however, on June 30, 1772, the business-like Nourse made Griffin and Goldsmith, on June 27, execute a regular legal document, in which Goldsmith assigned the copy formally to Griffin, and acknowledged receipt in full of the payment of £840. This document was three days later made over to Nourse, in the final transfer of the property to him. It is now the property of Mr W. M. Elkins, of Philadelphia.

Nourse did not accept Goldsmith's suggestion that Griffin be permitted to buy back part of the property in the work.

APPENDICES

I

To a PUPIL[1]

I have thought it adviseable, my dear young pupil, to adopt this method of giving my thoughts to you on some subjects which I find myself not well disposed to speak of in your presence, The reason of this you will yourself perceive in the course of reading this letter. It is disagreeable to most men, and particularly so to me, to say any thing which has the appearance of a disagreeable truth; and as what I have now to say to you is entirely respecting yourself, it is highly probable, that in some respect or other your views of things and mine considerably differ.

In the various subjects of knowledge which I have had the pleasure of seeing you study under my care, as well as those which you have acquired

---

1 From the *Scots' Magazine* for December, 1799 (LXI, 812), where it appeared with the heading, "Letter of the late Dr. Goldsmith." It was reprinted in the same magazine for December, 1801, and in Otridge's *Annual Register* for 1801. The MS. has never been seen, and the sponsor for its publication is not known. The content is inflated, and the style colourless and uncharacteristic. Its lack of genuineness cannot, however, be circumstantially proved.

under the various teachers who have hitherto much instructed you, the most material branch of information which it imports a human being to know, has been entirely overlooked, I mean the knowledge of yourself. There are indeed very few persons who possess at once the capability and the disposition to give you this instruction. Your parents, who alone are perhaps sufficiently acquainted with you for the purpose, are usually disqualified for the task, by the very affection and partiality which would prompt them to undertake it. Your masters, who probably labour under no such prejudices, have seldom either sufficient opportunities of knowing your character, or are so much interested in your welfare, as to undertake an employment so unpleasant and laborious. You are as yet too young and inexperienced to perform this important office for yourself, or indeed to be sensible of its very great consequence to your happiness. The ardent hopes and the extreme vanity, natural to early youth, blind you at once to everything within, and everything without, and make you see both yourself and the world in false colours. This illusion, it is true will gradually wear away as your reason matures and your experience increases; but the question is, what is to be done in the mean time? Evidently there is no plan for you to adopt, but to make use of the reason and experience of those who are qualified to direct you.

Of this however I can assure you, both from my own experience and from the opinions of all those whose opinions deserve to be valued, that if you aim at any sort of eminence or respectability in the eyes of the world, or in those of your friends; if you have any ambition to be distinguished in your future career, for your virtues, or talents, or accomplishments, this self-knowledge of which I am speaking, is above all things requisite. For how is your moral character to be improved, unless you know what are the virtues and vices which your natural disposition is calculated to foster, and what are the passions which are most apt to govern you? How are you to attain eminence in any talent or pursuit, unless you know in what particular way your powers of mind best capacitate you for excelling? It is therefore my intention, in this letter, to offer you a few hints on this most important subject.

When you come to look abroad into the world, and to study the different characters of men, you will find that the happiness of any individual depends not, as you would suppose, on the advantages of fortune or situation, but principally on the regulation of his own mind. If you are able to secure tranquillity within, you will not be much annoyed by any disturbance without. The great art of doing this, consists in the proper government of the passions. In taking care that no propensity is suffered to acquire so much power over your mind as to be the cause of immoderate uneasiness either to yourself or others. I insist particularly on this point, my dear young friend, because, if I am not greatly deceived, you are yourself very much disposed by nature to two passions, the most tormenting to the possessor, and the most offensive to others of any which afflict the human race; I mean pride and anger. Indeed, those two dispositions seem to be naturally connected with each other; for you have probably remarked, that most proud men are addicted to anger, and that most passionate men are also proud. Be this as it may I can confidently assure you, that if an attempt is not made to subdue those uneasy propensities now, when your temper is flexible, and your mind easy of impression, they will most infallibly prove the bane and torment of your whole life. They will not only destroy all possibility of your enjoying any happiness yourself, but they will produce the same effect on those about you; and by that means you will deprive yourself both of the respect of others, and the approbation of your own heart; the only two sources from which can be derived any substantial comfort or real enjoyment.

It is moreover a certain principle in morals, that all the bad passions, but especially those of which we are speaking, defeat, in all cases, their own purposes; a position, which appears quite evident on the slightest examination. For what is the

To A PUPIL

object which the proud man has constantly in
view? Is it not to gain distinction, and respect and
consideration among mankind? Now it is unfortunately the nature of pride to aim at this
distinction, not by striving to acquire such virtues
and talents as would really intitle him to it, but
by labouring to exalt himself above his equals by
little and degrading methods; by endeavouring,
for example, to outvie them in dress, or shew, or
expence, or by affecting to look down with
haughty superciliousness on such as are inferior
to himself, only by some accidental advantages,
for which he is in no way indebted to his own
merit. The consequence of this is, that all mankind
declare war against him; his inferiors, whom he
affects to despise, will hate him, and consequently
will exert themselves to injure and depress him;
and his superiors, whom he attempts to imitate,
will ridicule his absurd and unavailing efforts to
invade what they consider as their own peculiar
province.

If it may with truth be said that a proud man
defeats his own purposes; the same may, with
equal certainty, be affirmed of a man who gives
way to violence of temper. His angry invectives,
his illiberal abuse, and his insulting language,
produce very little effect on those who hear him,
and who perhaps only smile at his infirmities;
but who can describe the intolerable pangs of
vexation, rage, and remorse, by which the heart of

B   145   10

a passionate man is successively ravaged? Alas, it is himself alone, in whom the storm is pent up, who is torn by its violence, and not those against whom its fury is meant to be directed.

You will, I dare say, readily agree to the truth of all this; but you will perhaps be at a loss to conceive what can be my reasons for applying it to you. My principal reasons for thinking you subject to these unhappy failings, are very cogent; but they are of such a nature, that it is peculiarly painful for me to state them. In a word then, I have seen those hateful propensities govern you with such irresistible power, that they have overcome the strongest and most natural principle which can be supposed to reign in the heart of a young person; I mean the duty and affection you owe your parents. Surely it could be no common failing, no light or trivial fault of temper, that could be sufficient to counteract the warmest feelings and strongest duties of a young mind? duties and feelings so natural and so indispensable, that we justly conclude a young person who appears to be devoid of them, can scarcely possess any other valuable quality. From such grounds, then, can you think me harsh or uncharitable, if I have formed such conclusions?

I have been urged to what I have said by an earnest wish for the improvement of your character, and particularly for the amelioration of your heart. In a future letter I shall pursue the subject, by endeavouring to give you some rules respecting the government and improvement of the understanding. I hope and believe that your conduct will be such as to render any further admonitions on the subjects of this letter entirely unnecessary. I am, my dear pupil,

Yours, affectionately, &c.

II

To the Reverend THOMAS PERCY[1]

....I thank you for your trouble and advice, which shall be followed. I will wait at the Palace at two.

OLIVER GOLDSMITH

1 From Catalogue 70, November, 1895, of Wm Evarts Benjamin. The provenance of the letter is unknown, and the MS., although it has been traced to a sale in March, 1925, has not been available for examination.

I

To MRS. ANNE GOLDSMITH[1]

My Dear Mother,

If you will sit down and calmly listen to what I say, you shall be fully resolved in every one of those many questions you have asked me. I went to Cork and converted my horse, which you prize so much higher than Fiddleback, into cash, took my passage in a ship bound for America, and, at the same time, paid the captain for my freight and all the other expenses of my voyage. But it so happened that the wind did not answer for three weeks; and you know, mother, that I could not command the elements. My misfortune was that when the wind served I happened to be with a party in the country, and my friend the captain never inquired after me, but set sail with as much indifference as if I had been on board. The remainder of my time I employed in the city and its environs, viewing every thing curious, and you know no one can starve while he has money in his pocket.

[1] For a full discussion of the evidence which indicates that this letter is not genuine, see § 2 of the Introduction. It was first published by Prior, who believed it to be authentic, in his *Life*, in 1837. Prior's text is followed.

Reduced, however, to my last two guineas, I began to think of my dear mother and friends whom I had left behind me, and so bought that generous beast Fiddleback and bade adieu to Cork with only five shillings in my pocket. This to be sure was but a scant allowance for man and horse towards a journey of above an hundred miles; but I did not despair, for I knew I must find friends on the road.

I recollected particularly an old and faithful acquaintance I made at college, who had often and earnestly pressed me to spend a summer with him, and he lived but eight miles from Cork. This circumstance of vicinity he would expatiate on to me with particular emphasis.—"We shall," says he, "enjoy the delights of both city and country, and you shall command my stable and my purse."

However upon the way I met a poor woman all in tears, who told me her husband had been arrested for a debt he was not able to pay, and that his eight children must now starve, bereaved as they were of his industry, which had been their only support. I thought myself at home, being not far from my good friend's house, and therefore parted with a moiety of all my store; and pray, mother, ought I not to have given her the other half-crown, for what she got would be of little use to her?—However I soon arrived at the mansion of my affectionate friend, guarded by the vigilance of a huge mastiff, who flew at me and would have torn me to pieces, but for the assistance of a woman whose countenance was not less grim than that of the dog; yet she with great humanity relieved me from the jaws of this Cerberus, and was prevailed on to carry up my name to her master.

Without suffering me to wait long, my old friend, who was then recovering from a severe fit of sickness, came down in his night-cap, night-gown and slippers, and embraced me with the most cordial welcome, showed me in, and after giving me a history of his indisposition, assured me that he considered himself as peculiarly fortunate in having under his roof the man he most loved on the earth, and whose stay with him must, above all things, contribute to perfect his recovery. I now repented sorely I had not given the poor woman the other half-crown, as I thought all my bills of humanity would be punctually answered by this worthy man. I revealed to him my whole soul; I opened to him all my distresses; and freely owned that I had but one half-crown in my pocket, but that now, like a ship after weathering out the storm, I considered myself secure in a safe and hospitable harbour. He made no answer, but walked about the room, rubbing his hands, as one in deep study. This I imputed to the sympathetic feelings of a tender heart, which increased my esteem for him, and as that increased I gave the most favourable interpretation to his silence. I construed it into delicacy of sentiment, as if he dreaded to wound my pride by expressing his commiseration in words, leaving his generous conduct to speak for itself.

It now approached six o'clock in the evening, and as I had eaten no breakfast, and as my spirits were raised, my appetite for dinner grew uncommonly keen. At length the old woman came into the room, with two plates, one spoon, and a dirty cloth, which she laid upon the table. This appearance, without increasing my spirits, did not diminish my appetite. My protectress soon returned with a small bowl of sago, a small porringer of sour milk, a loaf of stale brown bread, and the heel of an old cheese all over crawling with mites. My friend apologised that his illness obliged him to live on slops, and that better fare was not in the house; observing at the same time that a milk diet was certainly the most healthful; and at eight o'clock he again recommended a regular life, declaring that for his part he would *lie down with the lamb and rise with the lark.* My hunger was at this time so exceedingly sharp that I wished for another slice of the loaf, but was obliged to go to bed without even that refreshment.

The lenten entertainment I had received made me resolve to depart as soon as possible; accordingly next morning, when I spoke of going, he did not oppose my resolution; he rather commended my design, adding some very sage counsel upon the occasion. "To be sure," said he, "the longer you stay away from your mother, the more you will grieve her and your other friends; and possibly they are already afflicted at hearing of this foolish expedition you have made." Notwithstanding all this, and without any hope of softening such a sordid heart, I again renewed the tale of my distress, and asking "how he thought I could travel above an hundred miles upon one half-crown?" I begged to borrow a single guinea, which I assured him should be repaid with thanks. "And you know, Sir," said I, "it is no more than I have often done for you." To which he firmly answered, "Why look you, Mr. Goldsmith, that is neither here nor there. I have paid you all you ever lent me, and this sickness of mine has left me bare of cash. But I have bethought myself of a conveyance for you; sell your horse and I will furnish you a much better one to ride on." I readily grasped at this proposal, and begged to see the nag, on which he led me to his bedchamber, and from under the bed he pulled out a stout oak stick. "Here he is," said he, "take this in your hand, and it will carry you to your mother's with more safety than such a horse as you ride." I was in doubt when I got it into my hand whether I should not, in the first place, apply it to his pate; but a rap at the street door made the wretch fly to it, and when I returned to the parlour, he intro-duced me, as if nothing of the kind had happened, to a gentleman who entered, as Mr. Goldsmith, his most ingenious and worth friend, of whom he had so often heard him speak with rapture. I could scarcely compose myself; and must have betrayed indignation in my mien to the stranger, who was a counsellor at law in the neighbourhood, a man of engaging aspect and polite address.

After spending an hour he asked my friend and me to dine with him at his house. This I declined at first, as I wished to have no further communication with my old hospitable friend; but at the solicitation of both I at last consented, determined as I was by two motives; one, that I was prejudiced in favour of the looks and manner of the counsellor; and the other, that I stood in need of a comfortable dinner. And there indeed I found every thing that I could wish, abundance without profusion, and elegance without affectation. In the evening when my old friend, who had eaten very plentifully at his neighbour's table, but talked again of lying down with the lamb, made a motion to me for retiring, our generous host requested I should take a bed with him, upon which I plainly told my old friend that he might go home and take care of the horse he had given me, but that I should never re-enter his doors. He went away with a laugh, leaving me to add this to the other little things the counsellor already knew of his plausible neighbour.

And now, my dear mother, I found sufficient to reconcile me to all my follies; for here I spent three whole days. The counsellor had two sweet girls to his daughters, who played enchantingly on the harpsichord; and yet it was but a melancholy pleasure I felt the first time I heard them; for that being the first time also that either of them had touched the instrument since their mother's death, I saw the tears in silence trickle down their father's cheeks. I every day endeavoured to go away, but every day was pressed and obliged to stay. On my going, the counsellor offered me his purse, with a horse and servant to convey me home; but the latter I declined, and only took a guinea to bear my necessary expenses on the road.

OLIVER GOLDSMITH

II

To EDMUND BURKE[1]

Tenple Exchange Coffee house near
Temple Bar Lond. Aug^st 15th 1757.

To Edmund Burke Esq.

Dear Sir

If you should ask why, in an interval of so many years, I have never written to you, permit me, Sir, to tell you that my long absence from

1 From the original.
The spurious character of the letter is demonstrated by the MS., of which the superscription and opening lines are a copy from a facsimile of Goldsmith's letter to Jane Lawder, published

England has prevent'd that happy intercourse which I years ago enjoy'd and from which I reap'd so much and so many benefits. Once more in my native land I should be glad to pay my respects to you, and to assure you how highly I should esteem the honour of a renewal of that friendship which in former times you deigned to honour me with. At the Coffee house, near the Bar, I am at present staying and when you respond to this, I shall hasten to you and in grasping your hand remember all the happy hours we have spent together and all the enjoyment I have deriv'd therefrom.

I have just seen Mr. Johnson and he sends his warmest regards to his friend and my friend.

From yr. obliged

OLIVER GOLDSMITH

in *Goldsmith's Miscellaneous Works* in 1858, by Charles Griffin, to whom the MS. of the letter then belonged. The engraver of the facsimile mistakenly executed "Tenple" for "Temple" in the heading, and the forger followed the error. Except in the copied lines, the handwriting bears no real resemblance to Goldsmith's. Various other details invalidate the letter, such as the unprecedented form of the salutation, accounted for by the fact that the forger's model had no salutation, and he was apparently too unfamiliar with eighteenth-century convention to supply a proper one. "Prevent'd" also shows ignorance of the usage governing the participial contraction. See also the following letters to Johnson (III and VI).

The subject-matter of the letter is cleverly unassailable, since the forger has taken advantage of the lack of information concerning the date of Johnson's first introduction to Goldsmith, and of the tradition of Burke's and Goldsmith's acquaintance at Trinity College, Dublin.

III

To SAMUEL JOHNSON[1]

Tenple Coffeehouse nr Tenple Bar

Octr 3. 1762.

My Dear Mr Johnson

Could you come round here this evening? I have at length concluded the Play, and shall entitle it She Stoops to Conquer subject to yr. better judgment. I should also be glad if you could advance me Ten guineas until I close with Mr Tonson, when amount shall be punctually repaid.

I saw Sir Joshua last Sunday. Had an attack of gout and melancholia, but smiled when he saw me and questioned me about that little difficulty. Trusting to see you about Seven this Evening

I am

Your Faithful

OLIVER GOLDSMITH

---

1 From a facsimile of the original, in the *Sphere*, for March 3, 1900. It is an unmistakable forgery, both in appearance and content. The misdating of *She Stoops to Conquer* by nine years alone suffices to condemn it. It appears to have been executed by the same hand as the preceding letter to Burke, and upon the same facsimile model for the heading. See also the second forged letter to Johnson (vi).

IV

To HENRY GOLDSMITH, J$_R$[1]

Temple, London Sept 30th 1766

My dear Henry

I seize the occasion of a friend's sailing this week for Nova Scotia to convey a small parcel of books which I trust will reach you safely. The bearer is a Mr Clarke of the Excise Office, who has been appointed to your corner of the world and who, being an old friend, will give you the latest intelligence concerning

Your affectionate Uncle

OLIVER GOLDSMITH

Mr H. Goldsmith
Annapolis Royal

[1] From the original. It is addressed "To Mr. Henry Goldsmith, Annapolis Royall, Nova Scotia," and on the verso of page one is a note, "Books by Uncle Oliver, 1766. H.G."

Both handwriting and content prove the letter a forgery. Henry Goldsmith, his nephew, to whom the letter is supposedly written, was only ten years old in 1766, and he did not go to America until after his uncle's death, in 1775 (*Notes and Queries*, 12, IV, 177). The handwriting is identical with that of the following letter to Henry Goldsmith, and with that of a forged copy of Goldsmith's *Stanzas on the Taking of Quebec*, which has appeared in several sales as a genuine autograph document. It bears no resemblance to Goldsmith's.

V

To HENRY GOLDSMITH, Jʀ¹

London June 7th 1768

My dear Henry

Your dear Father's death has afflicted me deeply—The news of this dreadful event only reached me yesterday and although I have already sent my love and condolence in a letter which you will see I pen this further line to my dear Nephew to express the hope that you and your Brother, young as you both are, will bear yourselves as the sons of such a man should—As to your future I shall not rest until I hit upon some means of serving you; and it may be that through the influence of some of my friends here you may procure a situation suited to your talents.

Meanwhile attend diligently to your studies, neglect nothing that can advance your interest when the opening occurs—Are you still inclined toward a military career? That would necessitate,

---

1 From the original. The letter has twice appeared in print as a genuine letter of Goldsmith's, first in Sir Ernest Clarke's *Family Letters of Oliver Goldsmith* (*Trans. Bib. Soc.* xv, 45), and then in W. H. Arnold's *Adventures in Book Collecting*, p. 143. Its spurious character is demonstrated by the handwriting and by the mistaken allusion to two sons. Henry Goldsmith had only two children, a son, Henry, and a daughter, Catherine.

besides a certain temper and constitution, a considerable sum of ready money—Something, however, might be managed abroad—in the Indies or
in America.

Let me hear from you, my dear Henry and with
love to you both Believe me,

Your affectionate Uncle

OLIVER GOLDSMITH

Mr. Henry Goldsmith
In care of Mrs. Hodson
 Athlone Ireland.

VI

To SAMUEL JOHNSON[1]

Tenple Coffeehouse nr. Tenple Bar
Dec. 2 1769.

Dear Mr Johnson

I am in great difficulties here summon'd for
a debt which is not actually due, and wh: I cannot
settle—at present at any rate—natheless I have
a Poem—"The Traveller"—nearly ready for the
Press.

1 From the original. This is a patent and clumsy forgery, both
in execution and content. The completion of *The Traveller* is
placed five years after it actually took place. The expression is
crude and entirely uncharacteristic. The handwriting, which
is similar to that of the preceding forged letters to Burke and
Johnson, bears no resemblance to Goldsmith's, and the same
facsimile model for the heading is again used.

Can you loan me a few pounds until such time
as I can dispose of my Manuscript? and obligd
yr. ever   Faithful Friend

OLIVER GOLDSMITH

VII

To HENRY BUNBURY[1]

Temple Exchange Coffee house near
Dear Sir,   Temple Bar Lond. July 18th 1773

I am very much obliged to you for your kind
invitation to Barton at which place I hope to be
by this day week at farthest. I should by this time
have been at yr hospitable hall comfortably
settled if I had not been dissapointed of of[2] sixty
pounds Mr Garrick kindly undertook to secure
me for my last literary effort. My health is shattered
by continual illness and my soul sickened by the

1 From the original. It is addressed, "To Mr. Bunbury, Barton,
St. Edmds. Bury Suffolk. Favor'd by Capt Greville."
   Handwriting, style, and content prove this letter a forgery.
The superscription of the Lawder letter is again used as a model,
although the hand is not that of the other copies. Neither does
it resemble Goldsmith's. Garrick's loan of £60 for the proposed
visit to Barton is placed in July, and it has now been shown
that this loan, and the visit, occurred in December of this year
(see Letters XLIX, L, and LI). The forger, as well as the other
forger who used the facsimile of the letter to Jane Lawder as
a model, seemed to be ignorant of the fact that Goldsmith
had used the Temple Exchange Coffee House only for a
temporary mailing address during 1757 and 1758.
2 *Sic.*

everlasting streets of this City now in the glare of an almost tropical sun so I assure you I long to roam in yr fields enjoying the beauties of nature and yr pleasing conversation. You ask me to copy the poem of mine shown to you by Captain Greville. My dear Bunbury how can I do so in one week which I fear will be too short for me to arrange my town affairs to admit of my journey to Barton? I hope to have it printed in October, if not published.

You will receive this within ten hours for which thank the Captain, My faithful postman. Believe me, my dear Bunbury, I long to be with you.

I am Dear Sir with the greatest esteem your most obedient humble Servant,

OLIVER GOLDSMITH

VIII

To MR. BOOTH[1]

If Mr Booth will send to Mr. Goldsmith Captain Brown's Book free of Expence, he will notice it after he has finished with his extracts from Hippesleys Book. In next Sundays Paper Captain Bs work is alluded to in reply to an article which appeared in the Dublin Evening Post.

1 From the original. The handwriting proves this letter a forgery. The only circumstance of the letter's content which definitely marks it as a forgery is the allusion to "next Sunday's paper." Sunday papers were not published during Goldsmith's period.

APPENDIX III

the Docter was born Novʳ ye 10 1729[2] at Pallace in the County of Longfoord near the seat of the Present Lord Annaly he was the Son of the Revᵈ Chaˢ Goldsmith Rector of Kilkenny West in the County Westmeath & Ann Jones Daughter to the Revᵈ Oliver Jones Rector of Elphin.

as to the Charactor of his father none cᵈ draw it better then himself in the Village Preacher in his Deserted Village which is none to be a just Picture of that Worthy man, he had seven Children viz 5 sons & 2 Daughters his Eldest the Revᵈ Henry Goldsmith to whom the Docter Dedicates his treveler remarkable for his polite Learning on whom the father formed his most sanguine hopes but he marrying at nineteen a Lady he liked left the College & retired to the Country and at his fathers Death possessed his Living.

The Docter the second son in his infancy was remarkably humorous but it was uncommon mostly to serious & reserved but when in Spirrits

---

1 The spelling and punctuation exactly reproduce the original, which forms part of the Goldsmith collection in the possession of Miss Constance Meade.

2 "9" has been heavily corrected to "8" in ink of a darker colour. In a contemporary copy which accompanies the MS. the date reads "1729."

none more agreeably so he was taken a most
perticular notice of by all the freinds of his family
who were all in the Church & found in him an
Early Genius for Learning & the muses, for at
the age of seven & eight he had a natural turn to
Ryhming that often amused his father and freinds
at that time he c^d hardly write legibly & yet he
was allways writting & allways burning what he
wrote, & to make these little annecdotes of his
life more regular I shall give any little occurance
I can recollect as the happen'd.

there was company at his fathers at that time
he was turnd of seven they were attended at tea
by a little boy who was desired to hand the
Kettle—but the handle being to hot the boy took
up the skirt of his coate to put between him & it
but unfortunately the Ladys perceived some thing
which made them Laugh immodarately whether
from the akwardness of the turn or any thing that
might be seen there I cant say but the Docter
immeadietly perceived there cause of Laughter
& informd his father who promised him a reward
of Gingerbread to write some thing on it and as
it was one of his earliest productions that can be
recollected tho perhaps not fit for the Publick
I shall insert it here

> Theseus did see as Poets say
> Dark Hell & its abysses
> But had not half so Sharp an Eye
> As our young Charming Misses

For they c^d through boys breeches peep
And view what ere he had there
It seemd to Blush & they all Laughd
Because the face was all Bare
   They laughed at that
Which some times Else
Might give them greatest pleasure
How quickly the c^d see the thing
Which was their darling treasure

   the Docter at this time was at School with the villiage Master whom he describes in his Poem he first gave him a taste for travail which he ever after lik^d, this man was a Quarter Master in Lord Galway's Regiment and serving many Champaigns with the Duke of Marlburrough came home & after a number of missfortunes was rewarded, with what, why was made a Country school master to a Country Parson this man read tolarably well for an Irish man & was employd by the Docters father for the early instruction of his children & those of all the Gentlemen in the neighbourhood tho he was severe on the D^r yet he was his greatest favourite & from him I realy beleive he first Learnd to despise fortune & feel more for every creature he saw in distress then for him self.

   at this time his fathers family increased by the Byrth of a third Son unexpected as his mother was for seven years without bearing a Child, this made the Father propose him for business in the Mercantile way as he thought his fortune to small to breed him & his Brother in the College & a younger family coming on his Brother was then at School with the Rev^d Mr Nelagin at Longford & the year following Entered Trinity College Dublin, however the D, being his mother greatest favourite she proposed giving him a liberal Education for a tradesman & as Mr Nelagin then retired to the Country the D was sent at eight to the Publick school of Elphin under the inspection & care of his uncle John Goldsmith Esqr who lived near the Town he there saw many of his freinds & was by them greatly Carressd who at that time thought him a Prodigy for his age nor was there any subject worth Olivers wit but he was obliged to exorcise it on.

one evening for a large Company of young people at his Uncles a young Gentleman playd the fiddle who thought him self a greater wit & humourist than any one Else did the Company insisted upon the Dr danceing a horn pipe which he refuse a long time but on the commands of his uncle he exibited he was then 9 years old & had lately had the small pox which left very deep red marks & he realy cut an ugly figure how ever he was a very good subject for the wit of our fiddleing Gentleman who Cryd out in rapture there was Esop how like Esop he was the very man by G, the D still danced for more then an hour till he fatagued our wit sufficiently who still kept on the Comparison of Esop with a very hearty Laugh at so bright a thought when the D stopt short & repeated these lines

The Herald proclaimed out then saying
See Esop Dancing & his Monkey playing

the Laugh turn^d against our Wit & the D was Embreaced by his uncle & got some sweetmeats which was always his reward by this time he made as great a progress in his school learning as one of his age c^d & it was then recommended to his father to have him fitted the College by all his freinds but in perticular by the Revd Thos Contarine his Fathers Brother in Law as none c^d be a better judge then this Gentleman being a man of most remarkable sence & universal Learing his father Chose rather to distress his younger Children & encourage his Genius by sending him to the College

He was therefore brought from Elphin & sent to Athlone which was within five miles of his fathers to Mr Campell who had set up in that Town & was reckonned a most ingenious Gentle man with him he continued two years till the employment not agreeing with Mr Campells health he was obliged to retire to the Country & the D was sent to the Revd Pat: Hughes Glergyman of Edgworths Town in the County of Longford here he was fitted for the College, & from his last journey from his fathers to this pleace he has I beleive taken the plot of his Play of the mistakes

of a night, for in his journy to this Town some
freind gave him a Guinea the Town was twenty
Miles from his fathers and he diverted the day
vewing the Gentlemens seats on the road &
night fell at a Village Call^d Ardagh, upon his
coming to the Village he enquired for the best
house in Town which he was shew'd upon his
riding to the door he Call^d for the Hostler who
appear^d he desired his horse might rubd waterd
and beated & very great care taken of him &
rushd in himself to a handsom Parlour where as
he thought sat the Landlord before a good fire
after the usual salutes he beleived a bottle of wine
c^d not be bad that cold night & let him also know
he had been fasting all day & to get some thing
comfortably good in a hurry for that he was very
hungry the man flew to obey his orders & immedietly a waiter with bottle & Glases appear^d
& he & his host sat to their bottle while it was
drinking the Man was inquisitive about his father
his pleace of Abode his name & famally upon his
information the man seem^d to be accquainted
with them & to treat him with great complisance
an Elegant Supper was immedietly served the
Company was the Host his wife & two Daughters
who were all pressing on Master Goldsmith to
sup he call^d affter two bottles more & insisted
on the Ladys telling their Choice for while the
Guinea lasted the Docter knew not how to spare
he was shew^d a very good Chamber where he

slept but before he parted desired Breakfast might be Early ready & the best in the house & bespoke a hot cake, which was all prepared before left his room, after breakfast he went to the Stable & had his horse dressd & oated & then went to the Land Lord & call^d for his Bill but how much was he confounded when the Gentleman told him he never kept an Inn a Mr Fanh F: & he was proud to have it in his power to enterain Mr Goldsmith son his dear Old freind & neighbour.

The June following 1743[1] the D was sent to the College & Entered under Mr Wilder, his temper was rather warm so was the D Wilder was the son of a neighbouring Gentleman and Mr Goldsmith requested a perticular care from him over his sons morals & behaviour as he was then but thirteen & a half, the D, then began to have a taste for the Sosiciety & as he was very pleasing he was invited by many he gave his accquaintance a dance & supper at his Chamber but unfortunately his Tutor heard of it who went imeadietly to his room & abused him most Greely & the Altercation ended in his Tutors giving him a box on the ear which he ever after resented

his first step was to dispose of the best of his Cloaths & he then left the College but spent a few days in the Citty till he spent the best part of what

1 "1743" is written between the lines in Mrs Hodson's hand, without a caret or other mark of punctuation.

mony he had & I have often heard him say he left Dublin with only a shilling in his Pocket he thought he c^d get Bread any where was fully resolved to go to Cork & take Shiping for he knew not where but he soon found his error for when his stock was spent which he husbanded for three days he was then obliged to sell his shirts waist coat and any other little things he had about him for a support his shoes were worn out & he was then eighty miles from Dublin & about forty from his fathers house without Cloaths Shoes or a penny in his Pockett, he then to Late began to think of what he had done & as the Prodgal son returnd to his father after suffering all that naked-ness & famine c^d endure & he has told me a handfull of Grey pease he got from a Girl at a weak as he passed through the Country was the most Comfortable repast he ever made after fasting 24 hours, within a few miles of his fathers house he wrote to his Brother who fitted him out again & brought him to Dublin & at least out-wardly reconciled him to his Tutor from this the D wod fall into many little extravagances when ever he got a remtance from the country he liv'd well but still was calld a good Idle Scholar but never pleased his Tutor who imagined was rather convinced he c^d do much more then he did how ever he got all the Honnours of the College for his standing.

I now must request the reader will read himself

in the Character of the Man in Black in the Citizen of the world he there gives an account of his Fathers Death which I w^d wish to ommit & many other incidents of his life as I am sertain that Charector is his own.

after his Fathers Death he was taken a perticular notice of by his Uncle Contrine who w^d have him persue his studdys & brought him to him self where he asisted[1] till he took his degree he then w^d have him read for orders & w^d have given him Bread, but this he never liked for his inclination led him to Travail but Condescending to his Uncles desire he did read for Orders and waited on Bishop Sing at Elphin & answerd Examinaton the Bishop asked his age which he told was twenty and his Lord Ship said he must wait till he was of a proper age for it was thought his Lordship designd his uncles living for another as he was that time an old man his Uncle got him at that time a Tuition at a Gentlemans family in the Neighbourhood where he lived a year but he never liked confinement at the end of this year he made an excursion to Munster & brought with him a handsome horse and about thirty pound in his pocket he stay'd about six weeks away and all his freinds concluded he had left the Kingdom but he returnd to his mothers without a penny upon a little horse worth about eighteen shillings which he call^d Fiddle Back his Mother was much

1 Here is scratched out, "him with his Mother."

concern^d at his folly & c^d not be readily reconcild to him, but his Brother & Sisters so contrived to meet at his Mothers to bring on a reconciliaton & after many cool repremands on her side She insisted on where he had been where he had spent his money horse linnen &c. as he brought nothing home but what was on his back,

he then told his mother if she c^d cooly sit down & listen he wd resolve the many Questions askd he informd us he had been in Cork that he had sold his horse & paid for his passage to a Captian of an American Ship but the winds did not answer for three weeks during which time he saw every thing curious in & about the City of Cork that he had met some accquaintance & that he did not know how to starve with mony in his Pockett that unfortunatly the day the wind served he hapened to be on a party in the Country with some freinds & his friend the Captian never enquired after him he stayd in Cork while he c^d stay till the last two Guineas forty shillings of which he gave for Fiddle Back & then had but a Crown[1] to bring him home, which was rather little for himself & horse for a hundred & twenty mile but on his laveing the City he recollected a fathfull freind & accquaintance he had in the College & who often most earnestly press^d him to go & spend a Summer with him at his Seate within eight mile

1 A note to this appears at the foot: "1 guinea is 2*l*. 5*s*. 6*d*. Irish." Two guineas is obviously meant.

of Cork that they w^d have the pleasures of the
city & that Dr Oliver sh^d command his house &
purse which was ever at his service, he had but
two half crowns & on his being two miles from
Town he met a poor Woman with eight little
clean Children She was all in Tears & told him
a long melocholy tale that her husband was that
morning seiged for a Debt he had not to pay &
that he was draged to Jayle & that the Labour
of his hands was the only suport she had for them
eight Children, the Docter redily devided his
stock with her for he had his freind to apply to
from whom he c^d get money ennough to carry
him home at length he arrived at his freinds house
all the marks of snugness about it not forgeting
a large mastiff who had like to tear him to peices
upon his going in but was releived by an old Grim
looking woman whom he askd for his freind &
sent in his name his freind flew to embreace &
hoped he was then come to perform the many
promisses he had made of spending the sumer
with him the D tould he sh^d know more of that
shortly, his freind was only recovering from a
severe fit of Illness in his night Gown cap &
slippers & gave the D a long detail of his disorder,
but how happy was he then to have the man he
most loved on Earth to help his recoery asked him
whether he had then come from Dublin or his
mothers happy was my poor D to have so faithfull
a freind to lay open his distresses to & informd

him of every thing that had happen^d him since he left his freinds that he was now returning with but half a Crown in his Pocket, but upon his recolecting him, his dear freind, it made him quiet easy he returnd no answer but walkd about & rubd his hands in short the time of dineng was come the D grew hungry & impeatiaently waited for dinner which he saw no prospect of till six oClock when the old woman appeard with 2 pleates & a spoon & Cloath which She laid on a table which renewd the D spirrits & up She brought a very small bowl of Segoe a small poranger of bad sower milk & a peice of bad brown bread he invited the D to eat & highly recomended a milk Diet for his part he was Confined to such Slops as this thrusting a spoonfull into the D mouth the D lookd but sower at his entertainment but had he ennough of even what he got he wd have been pleased, at eight a Clock his freind recomended a regular life that for his part to lye with the lamb & rise with the Lark was what he wd recommend to his freinds the D stomack was greater for another peice of his bread & milk but he was obliged to acquese & go to bed

in the morning he was resolved to borrow a Guinea & go of for his freinds living he did not like but when he mentiond his going of, why truly to be sure he had given his mother & freinds high offence at his foolish ramble that the longar he stayd from them the greater their anger must be,

and that he would advize him by all means to go
home with all expedition, but S^r says the D you
know my ability to travial on half a Crown more
then a hundred miles now if you lend me a Guinea
I will remit it to you & return you many thanks
& you know S^r tis what I often done for   , why
look you Mr Goldsmith that is neither here nor
there, all the money I have ever borrowd from
you you know I have paid you & this dam^d sickness of mine it has taken a way all my Cash, but
I have found out an easie method for your going
home, how pray S^r says the D why sell your horse
& I will lend you one and pray S^r says the D
shew me the horse you intend to lend me with
that he brought him to his bed Chamber which
the D thought a strange pleace for a horse & from
under his bed he brought him out an oak stick
& said that was it, the D took it in his hand look^d
earnestly at it & then at him & had it just redy
drawn to give him a great beating when a loud
wrap at the street door made the freind fly to it
& introduce into the parlour a Gentleman dressd
in mourning of a most pleasing aspect whom he
introduced to the D, a Councelor F. G. & the D
to him as his worthy & ingenious freind Mr Goldsmith of whom he had so often heard him spake
with rapture, the D all this while walked about the
room rubbing his hands biteing his lips & giving
his freind many angry looks till the subject was
cheanged by the polite Conversation of the Coun-

celor, after spending an hour the Councelor
invited the D & his freind to Dine with him at his
sate which the D declined for some time but he
was pressd by both that he waited on the Councelor
for two reasons first because he liked the councelor
& secondly he wanted a dinner as he had not eat
nothing but bread & Milk[1] since he left Cork, at
the Counselors he found every thing neat and
elegan a Most beautifull place there ware two
lovely Daughters which the Counselor introduc.d
to the D.r the spent a Most agreeable evening his
Friend desir.d him to prepare for home, the
counselor who had observd the many sower looks
the D.r had given him insisted on Mr Goldsmiths
spending a few days with him he prest so earnestly
that the D.r was at last oblig.d to declare he wod
not stir a step with the dam.d paltroon and
desird him to goe home and be sure the next day
you goe abroad dont forget y.e Horse our Gentleman went of with a Sneer and left the D.r to inform
the Counselor of his tratement of him, who laught
hartily and at the same time told Mr Goldsmith
he believ.d M.r H. was a verry grate scounderle,
the Ladies brought the D.r to the Gardens where
the amus.d themselvs playing a bouls and at Night
they playd the Harpsicord and sung, the D.r
Observ.d the Counselor drown.d in Tears on hearing
Ladys sing and p[lay] which he beg.d M.r Gold-

1 Here the handwriting changes to Maurice's, who evidently
wrote the remainder at Mrs Hodson's dictation.

smith wod excuse; since it had been their first time to play or sing since the Death of their Mother & of his Wife, but that he wish<u>d</u> in any respect they cod be pleasing to him, the next day the D<u>r</u> attempted to go but the Conselor wod by no means hear of it and told him he sho<u>d</u> have a good Hors and servant at his Service, the D<u>r</u> spent three days with him and at his goeing the Counselor offerd him his purse and Insisted he sh<u>d</u> take what he wanted also a Horse and Servant however he took three half Guineas but posotivly refus<u>d</u> the Counselors Horse

And now D<u>r</u> Mother says he since I have struggeld so hard to come home to you why are you not better pleas<u>d</u> to see me, and pray says the Mother have you ever wrote a letter of thanks to that dear good man since you came home, no says the D<u>r</u> I have not then says the Mother you are an ungratefull Savage a Monster in short the whole boddy of his Friends which ware present up braid<u>d</u> him for which he for a full half houre sat listning to with grate composure and after they had vented their Passion he beg<u>d</u> they wod sit down and compos themselv<u>s</u> for what he told them was only to amuse them and that there was not one word in it; how ever he afterward assur<u>d</u> me of its veracity

After this he did not know well what to do with himself for to return to his Tuition he wod not, he liv<u>d</u> som time with his Sister Hodson before he

176

wod attempt to see his Uncle Contrine but soon a reconciliation was brough on Mr. and Mr^s Lawder his Uncles daughter who was verry fond of him and a particular Friend

His Uncle and Friends then Concluded to send him to the Temple and had his name enter^d they then acquipt him handsomly he accordingly set of for Dublin on his way to London but unfortunatly met a Mr. S. at a Coffie house they both fell into play and los every shill^g of fivty Pound so once more return^d to his Mother a hart broken dejected being twas then he began to [repen]t of his past misconduct and if he was once more taken notice of [promised to] behave with more circumspection for the future, they then desir^d him he migh prepair for the studdy of physick and once More his Good Uncle was reconsil^d to him at lenth he was sent to Edinburg and in 1753 enter^d that College From this date I am a Stranger to what happn^d him he wrote several letters to his Friends from Switzerland Germany and Italy for six years[1] [   ].

1 The last line, beginning with "six," is scored out. Only the first two words are decipherable.

LIST OF CORRESPONDENTS

INDEX

References to the notes are in italics.

INDEX

Goldsmith, Maurice, letter to, 83; crosses out passages in early letters, xix, *54, 61*; acts as Goldsmith's executor, xxiii; receives legacy, xx, 85; proposes to visit Goldsmith, xix, 54; journeys to London, xx, *89, 90*; writes part of Mrs Hodson's narrative, *175*; mentioned, x, xiv, xvii, *59*

GOLDSMITH, OLIVER, recalls *adventures* of youth, 37; plans to recount *adventures*, 46, 93; likened to *Aesop*, 165; *affection* for family, ix; *age*, 57; introduces Dr *Andrews*, 122; working on *Animated Nature*, 96, 112; plans to extend *Animated Nature*, 137; *apologizes* to Garrick, 77; *appearance*, 57, 58; adventure at *Ardagh*, 167–8; *arrested* at Newcastle, 20; threatened with *arrest*, 66; dignity of *authorship*, 51; "*avarice* true ambition*," 61; invited to *Barton*, 129; plans visit to *Barton*, 128; *birth*, 162; *borrows* money, 73, *75*, 126–7; feeling for brother *Charles*, xviii; hears from *Charles*, 91; unable to help *Charles*, xvi; inquires about *Charles*, xvii, 31, 54, 87; tries to buy *Chatterton* MSS, *100*; shows *Chinese* erudition, 39; plans *Citizen of the World, 39*; friendship for Lord *Clare*, xxi; enters *college*, 168; triumphs over *Colman*, xlix; plans unwritten *comedies*, 95, 127; debt to Uncle *Contarine*, 16, 170; mentions Uncle *Contarine's* illness, 46; reconciled to Uncle *Contarine*, 177; finds *Continent* dull, 94; writes prologue for *Cradock*, 106; *death*, xxiii; *debts*, xxiii, *20, 32, 66, 75*,

96, 117, 126; *destitution* on the Continent, xiv, 26; plans *Dictionary of Arts and Sciences*, 123; "*different* from rest of mankind*," 43; escapes *drowning*, 21; studies at *Edinburgh*, 3, 5, 14; expenses at *Edinburgh*, 3, 4, 7, 16; describes his professors at *Edinburgh*, 5–6; lives in seclusion at *Edinburgh*, 5, 13; advice on *education*, 59; early *education*, 164–6; uses *experiences* in his fictions, xxiv, xxix; literary *fame*, xxi; prophesies his own *fame*, 38–40; inquires for *family* and *friends*, 14, 17, 31, 53, 55, 63, 87, 95, 96; character of *father*, x, 162; recounts adventures on *Fiddleback*, xxv-vi, 170–6; "*folly* a proof of regard*," 65; plans to visit *France*, 14; visits *France*, 91; London *friends*, 50, 51, 86; adopts maxims of *frugality*, 45; lives in a *garret*, 40; thanks Colman for taking *Good-Natured Man*, 74; withdraws *Good-Natured Man* from Garrick, 76–7; plans to revive *Good-Natured Man*, 126; describes Duchess of *Hamilton*, 12; visits Duke of *Hamilton*, 17–18; visits *Highlands*, 7–8; ridicules *himself*, 13, 40; writes about *himself*, 54; abridges *History of England*, 105; writes a *History of England* for Dodsley, 73; revises *History of England*, 124; aids William *Hodson*, xxii, 88–90, 99–102, 114; indebtedness to *Hogarth*, 41; compares *Holland* and Scotland, 24–5; describes *Holland*, 21–4; friendship for *Hornecks*, xv, 80, 92, 96, 128; rejected as *hospitalmate*, xxx; *illness*, 71, 72;

183

Malone, Edmond, xxiv, 42
Mann, Sir Horace, *86*
Marana, *L'Espion Turc*, *5*
Marchi, Giuseppe Filippo Liberati, *86*
Marlborough, Duke of, 164
Marlowe, young, xl
Martin, Mrs, in Green Arbour Court, *62*
March, Lord, 99
Mason, Wm Shaw, *Statistical Survey of Ireland*, *9*
Mason, Mr, *42*
Matilda, Queen, *123*
Mattei, Signora Columba, 29
McArdle, James, *64*
McDermott, Mrs, *9*
Meade, Miss Constance, xl, *8, 19, 32, 49, 56, 78, 83, 91, 98, 102, 112, 113, 115, 120, 162*
Memoirs of a Protestant, xvi
Memoirs of My Lady B, *51, 69*
Middlesex, 30
Millot, Claude-François-Xavier, *Histoire d'Angleterre*, 125
Mills, Edward, letter to, 32; mentioned, 56
Mills, Mrs, 33
Milner, Rev. Dr John, 68
Mitford, Rev. John, *xlviii*
Monro, Alexander, 5
Montaigne, 65
Monthly Review, xvi, *66, 67*
Morgan, J. P., Library, *129*
Morris, Mr, *74*
Moser, Mary, *81*
Munster, Goldsmith's expedition to, 170
Murphy, Arthur, xliii, *50*, 119

Nelagin, Mr, Henry Goldsmith's teacher, 165
Nesbitt, Mr, 81
Newbery, Francis, 126, 127
Newbery, John, letters to, 71, 72; mentioned, *75*

Newcastle-upon-Tyne, 20
Newton, A. Edward, *18, 117*
Newton, Isaac, 46
New York Public Library, *76*
Nichols, John, the publisher, xxxiii
Northamptonshire, 79
Northcote, James, *Life of Sir Joshua Reynolds*, xviii; mentioned, *135*
Northumberland, Duke of, letters to, 113, 120
Northumberland-house, letter to, 79
Notes and Queries, 29, *58, 108, 157*
Nourse, John, letters to, 122, 136; mentioned *124*
Nova Scotia, *58*
Nugent, Hon. Lieut.-Col., xxii, 99, 100
Nugent, Robert (Lord Clare) xxi, 96, *99, 106*
Nugent, Thomas, *The Grand Tour, 21*

Odonogh, Mr, 114
Old Bayley, *62*, 133
Otway, Thomas, 46

Padua, xiii
Pallas, 31, 162
Panter, W. G., *121*
Paris, letter from, 92; Goldsmith intends to visit, 15, 16
Parr, Remigius, *64*
Peckham School, *68*
Pennick, Rev. Richard, letters to, 108, 110
Pennsylvania Historical Society, *122*
Percy, Mrs Anne, letter to, 78; dines with Goldsmith, *112*; mentioned, 80
Percy, Rev. Thomas, letters to, 79, 115, 147; alters Goldsmith's epilogue, xliv–vii; at Alnwick,

INDEX